LEADING YOUR STUDENTS IN WORSHIP

PRAISE FOR *LEADING YOUR STUDENTS IN WORSHIP*...

Worship leaders! Create the environment that involves rather than performs. Jim Marian has written an accessible, practical, nuts-and-bolts resource book that is must reading for any dedicated song/worship leader.

Yohann Anderson
Songs and Creations, Inc.

Jim Marian shows us what youth ministry in this decade must look like.

Jim Burns
National Institute of Youth Ministry

Jim Marian has written an informative and practical book to give youth workers the confidence and tools they need to teach their students how to worship. By following Jim's suggestions, you'll be taking giant steps forward in effective, meaningful times for you, your kids, and your programs.

Tommy Coomes
Maranatha! Music

Jim Marian has given all of us in youth ministry a wonderful resource with his book *Leading Your Students in Worship*. Get it! Read it! Use it! Your youth group meetings will be transformed into celebrations, and your students will fall in love with their Creator!

Wayne Rice
Youth Specialties

LEADING

YOUR

STUDENTS

IN

WORSHIP

HOW TO PLAN AND LEAD DYNAMIC SINGING TO HELP STUDENTS GROW CLOSER TO GOD

JIM MARIAN

▼ VICTOR BOOKS

A DIVISION OF SCRIPTURE PRESS PUBLICATIONS INC.
USA CANADA ENGLAND

All Scripture quotations, unless otherwise indicated, are from the *New American Standard Bible*, © the Lockman Foundation, 1960, 1962, 1963, 1968, 1971, 1972, 1973, 1975, 1977. Used by permission. All rights reserved.
Scripture quotations marked NIV are from the HOLY BIBLE, NEW INTERNATIONAL VERSION®. Copyright © 1973, 1978, 1984 by International Bible Society. Used by permission of Zondervan Bible Publishers. All rights reserved.

Verses marked TLB are taken from *The Living Bible*, © 1971 Tyndale House Publishers, Wheaton, IL 60189. Used by permission.

ISBN 1-56476-086-3

Cover Design: Joe DeLeon

Produced by the Livingstone Corporation. David R. Veerman, J. Michael Kendrick, Steve Benson, and Tan Nguyen, project staff.

C ONTENTS

DEDICATION

TO MY PRECIOUS WIFE, LYNNE,
WHO FIRST INTRODUCED ME TO THE JOY OF
WORSHIPPING THE LORD
THROUGH PRAISE AND WORSHIP.

F O R E W O R D

Jim Marian joins the growing chorus of voices in what many believe to be the most important renewal of the twentieth century—the rediscovery of worship.

First came the liturgical renewal—a result of the publication, promulgation, and implementation of the *Constitution on the Liturgy*. Fast on its heels was the bursting forth of the charismatic movement with its freedom, spontaneity, and openness to the Spirit. And then, 20 years ago, the praise and worship movement arose out of the night to bring new light and a change of heart and life to the hippies who soon became part of the Jesus movement and the worship renewal it engendered.

While these renewal movements lit flames of fire here and there around the world, evangelicals remained largely untouched by the movement. But now in recent years evangelicals are beginning to rediscover the power of worship to change lives and communities, and here is where *Leading Your Students in Worship* fits into the picture.

Marian wisely recognizes that young people are drawn into worship through singing. But he also knows that good singing, that is, singing that is both socially enjoyable and spiritually transforming, does not come automatically. It takes understanding, work, and the development of the worship leadership gift.

Consequently *Leading Your Students* in Worship is full of highly practical and extremely useful insights and resources on both the "why" and the "how to" of leading youth in singing and worship.

I commend *Leading Your Students in Worship* as a valuable resource and guide for all who lead the young. For this is a book that deals not only with singing, but also with the spiritual maturation of those who sing.

Robert Webber

I N T R O D U C T I O N

Worship to me is a time that I feel I am the closest to my Lord, which strengthens my walk with Him and encourages me to stay strong because He is the only way, hope, and future, and He will always be there. Through the songs we sing I remember that.
Ellen—10th grade

Through more than a decade of youth ministry, I have yet to encounter a book for youth workers on the subject of leading students in singing and worship. Why? Perhaps it's because a book on how to lead singing is a lot like a book on how to swim; it's not real practical until you just plain get out and do it! Yet you have to start somewhere. I began my music ministry with youth years ago out of a desperate need to provide my students with more than simply a song session. I was compelled to bring my students into very real and meaningful experiences with God in worship through singing.

As a floundering young youth pastor seeking resources on the subject, I found few. Several books on the subject of Christian worship were helpful, as were those rare seminars held on the subject of youth singing. Some good youth songbooks provided me with helpful material, too. Perhaps the most helpful resources were more experienced worship leaders who were kind enough to show me the ropes. However, I know that not everyone is fortunate enough to have a teacher or mentor in the area of youth worship.

The path of trial and error, endless time and practice, broken strings and mistakes galore finally brought me to a point where I was able to lead the students in my youth ministry in meaningful singing and worship. Over the years, this experience has given me an understanding of youth worship and a philosophy of worship leading that I have been able to share with others. Much of this experience, both philosophical and practical, is here in these pages.

My hope is that this book will enable you to develop your own convictions regarding youth worship, so that you may challenge and draw your students into a closer walk with their Lord. I also trust that you will find some very practical tools and ideas to aid you in the process. Finally, I believe that it is God's will that we be worshiping ministries. That includes our youth groups. While singing may not be the only way for teens to worship God, I believe it to be one of the most effective and rewarding forms of worship. Youth worship through singing not only blesses our Lord, but it blesses His children as they learn to praise Him.

PART ONE

DEVELOPING A PHILOSOPHY OF YOUTH SINGING AND WORSHIP

H ave your students ever asked why your youth group sings so much? Does your church board have a hard time understanding why you requested so much money for a new sound system for the youth room? Have you ever noticed the differences between junior high and senior high singing and worship? Have you ever wondered why some worship leaders are more effective than others? Do you have a clear understanding of what *worship* really is?

These are all practical questions that can be answered if you have considered a philosophy of youth singing and worship. Since you're reading this book, I'm sure you have an interest in the subject and are open to investigating the biblical principles and practical applications that are necessary for providing your students with a meaningful worship ministry.

Rather than jumping right into the practical "tips and tools" of song and worship leading, I believe it is wise to establish a reason or philosophy for doing what we do. The information contained in the next four chapters should provide you with a firm foundation upon which to build your worship ministry.

1

MAKING WORSHIP A PRIORITY
IN YOUR MINISTRY

My relationship with God has gotten a lot better over the past few years. I know that singing has had a big part in that because I can just say out loud to everyone how I feel in those songs. I close my eyes and lift my voice and all the words in the songs make so much sense and are put so beautifully so we can sing and praise the Lord.

Stacy—9th grade

Worshipping God through song is, for me, the most effective way I worship.

Brandon—11th grade

Sure, I can laugh now. But as I look back to that early "worship" experience, lifeless and void as it was, it was pretty scary! I sat in the back of the room that Sunday morning, observing what was to become my first ministry. The group of eleven high-school students looked about as excited to sing God's praises as they might have been to have their braces tightened.

But honestly, what did they have to be excited about? I knew that their nice Sunday School teacher was doing her best to lead the kids in singing, but she was striking out.

Teetering precariously atop an old wooden stool, she peered nervously through her Coke-bottle glasses at the microscopic chords in a tattered songbook on the floor below her. She never looked up, never smiled, only yelled out occasionally, "OK, let's hear ya!" and "One more time!" The incessant rhythm of the strum coming from her toy-like guitar reminded me of Chinese water torture.

The poor kids who were being subjected to this torment calmly responded by not responding at all. Some kids passed notes, some stared at the clock, while others simply drifted off into space as they contemplated which fast food restaurant they would coerce their parents into taking them to for lunch.

Call it what you will, but as I sat regarding this sorry scene, I felt a stirring, yes, a calling, to teach these young people how to worship God. There were only a few problems. One, I had never led singing before, and two, I didn't play an instrument. Undaunted, I went by faith to the local music store and purchased a guitar for $250 without knowing a single note.

Although as a high-school student I was probably no more interested in worship than these students, I had become convicted of God's desire for His people to be worshippers. I was convinced that young people, when properly led and motivated, could worship God with enthusiasm and depth through singing. Since then, I have tried to consistently make worship a priority in my ministry to young people, and I have been amazed at the ways God has chosen to bless it.

One of my favorite characters in church history, Martin Luther, was also dedicated to the priority of worship through singing. In fact, next to the Scriptures, Luther believed the hymnbook was the most important book for the church. He once proclaimed, "To know God is to worship Him." Luther also insisted that worship was not an option for the godly person, but an essential act of Christian expression. The opportunity to worship publicly had not always been available. In fact, for more than a century during the Middle Ages, congregational singing was forbidden in the church. Luther reacted against this ban (among other church practices) during the Reformation in the 16th century. "Let God speak directly to His people through the Scriptures," he argued, "and let His people respond with grateful songs of praise." Luther himself composed 37 hymns of praise and worship, many of which are still sung today.[1]

For the great reformer, worship through singing was a priority not to be taken lightly. Yet, in many cases, we don't give this divine privilege its proper emphasis in our churches and youth ministries today. Perhaps for this reason A. W. Tozer once proclaimed, "Worship is the missing jewel in modern evangelicalism."[2]

Where is worship among the priorities in your youth ministry? Has it become a "missing jewel"? Perhaps it's time to start digging.

PUTTING THE CART BEFORE THE HORSE

Traditionally, youth workers have concentrated their efforts on a variety of programs and ministries. For example, some groups build their programs around discipleship. Other ministries stress outreach, some stress activities, while others emphasize service and social action.

I know of one youth worker in my area who is committed to providing his students with "serious" Bible study. Not only does he have attendance requirements, but the group is on a program of Bible reading and memory work that would make most seminarians' heads spin! Of course, Bible study is essential, even pivotal in a balanced and effective youth ministry. However, not many youth workers would give worship equal or preeminent standing among other spiritual endeavors, when in fact, it's foundational.

"Putting the cart before the horse"? This age-old saying poses an important question about our youth ministries. Are we pushing students into service and leadership because we hope it will spark their love for God? Or are we challenging them to grow in their adoration of God, and then allowing this inward commitment to fuel their desire to serve and lead?

Donny was a student in my youth group who loved to be at everything we offered. That was great, but unfortunately once he was there, he always chose to distract rather than participate. He talked during worship and Bible study and never got serious during our small-group times. Understandably, I cringed when I discovered that Donny had signed up for an all-day outreach to a group of orphans in Mexico. On the one hand I admired his interest (I mean, this kid could have spent all day playing Nintendo or something), but on the other, I suspected that Donny's heart wasn't really right for this trip.

Unfortunately, my gut-level instinct proved correct. Not only did

Donny show a lack of respect for the many cultural differences, but he even demonstrated insensitivity to the orphans, teasing several of them inappropriately. Donny was spiritually immature, and it showed. But in the final analysis, I don't think Donny failed because he couldn't express Christ's love to the orphans; he failed because he had never learned to express his own love for Christ. The desire to sincerely serve God needed to come from within.

Many times students like Donny are thrown into areas of service and involvement before they've learned to simply love and experience God for themselves. I have found over the years that teaching young people how to worship is the most effective tool for encouraging personal devotion to God.

Jim Burns, a veteran youth worker, recognizes the necessity of a strong worship emphasis. He states in his book *The Youth Builder:* "One of the main goals of a good youth ministry program should be to develop an understanding of, and enthusiasm for, worship. When the groundwork has been laid effectively and the students have developed the skills to worship God, then young people can have a regular and meaningful worship experience.[3]

LOVE THE LORD YOUR GOD . . .
In order for worship to make an impact on the lives of your students, it has to be given priority. In the book of Psalms, it is clear that David recognized the importance of praise and worship. His personal devotion and love for the Lord was passionate and expressive. From his heart flowed songs and poems that reflected his relationship with God. For example, consider Psalm 95:1-7:

> O COME, let us sing for joy to the Lord;
> Let us shout joyfully to the rock of
> our salvation.
> Let us come before His presence with thanksgiving;
> Let us shout joyfully to Him with psalms.
> For the Lord is a great God,
> And a great King above all gods,
> In whose hand are the depths of the earth;
> The peaks of the mountains are His also.
> The sea is His, for it was He who made it;

And His hands formed the dry land.
Come, let us worship and bow down;
Let us kneel before the Lord our Maker.
For He is our God,
And we are the people of His pasture,
and the sheep of His hand.

Reminding youth of the Psalms is not the only way to encourage them to worship in deeper and more meaningful ways. Perhaps the strongest case for establishing a worship emphasis comes from the greatest commandment, found in Mark 12:28-31. A scribe asked Jesus what commandment was foremost, and He answered, "You shall love the Lord your God with all your heart, and with all your soul, and with all your mind, and with all your strength."

The most critical action we can take in our ministries is to encourage students to love God in a personal way, before making them youth group presidents, young theologians, or sending them on a summer mission to Zimbabwe. These things, to be sure, are important and will come in time. In fact, they will naturally flow out of the student's life as he or she continues to mature in his or her Christian walk.

In his book *Celebration of Discipline,* Richard Foster writes, "The divine priority is worship first, service second. Our lives are to be punctuated with praise, thanksgiving, and adoration. Service flows out of worship. Service as a substitute for worship is idolatry. Activity may become the enemy of adoration."[4]

As I've ministered to students over the years, I've observed that those who take leadership in worship take leadership in other areas of spiritual growth and service. These things, then, are the natural outgrowth of a heart immersed in the love of God. For Jesus goes on to say, "The second [greatest commandment] is this, 'You shall love your neighbor as yourself.' There is no other commandment greater than these" (Mark 12:31).

WHY SINGING?
You may be thinking, *There are a lot of ways to worship God. Why is singing so important?* Good question. Let's consider several reasons.

First, there is a tremendous biblical precedent for singing in the praise and worship of God. I've already mentioned a couple of passages. Here is a sampling of other passages that reinforce this principle:

> Through Him then, let us continually offer up a sacrifice of praise to God, that is, the fruit of lips that give thanks to His name. (Hebrews 13:15)

> But about midnight Paul and Silas were praying and singing hymns of praise to God, and the prisoners were listening to them. (Acts 16:25)

> Praise the LORD!
> For it is good to sing praises to our God;
> For it is pleasant and praise is becoming. (Psalm 147:1)

> Praise the LORD!
> Sing to the Lord a new song,
> And His praise in the congregation of the godly ones.
> (Psalm 149:1)

> Let the word of Christ richly dwell within you, with all wisdom teaching and admonishing one another with psalms and hymns and spiritual songs, singing with thankfulness in your hearts to God. (Colossians 3:16)

Second, music is the "universal language"—a medium that can communicate and influence people from all walks and stages of life. We know that people can routinely quote the lyrics to songs they learned 10 or 20 years ago, and you already know how much your young people are influenced by the music they listen to. So much of it is negative, but students are also very receptive to the positive uses of music in worship. Kids are natural singers. When encouraged and taught, they can become natural worshippers as well.

Third, worship promotes group participation and community. The experience can, in many cases, draw a group together while tearing down individual walls of inhibition and fear. Singing encourages this kind of closeness like no other aspect of youth ministry. Eric Heard, youth pastor at First Evangelical Free Church in Fullerton, California agrees. He claims that "not only is unity built through group singing, but the normally 'competitive' atmosphere among the students is broken down."

Finally, worship provides one of the few opportunities we give our youth to focus completely on unselfish giving to God. As youth workers we often strive to provide our students with personal attention. We encourage times to share and pray for needs and burdens. We also implement programs where learning, growth, and Christian service are emphasized. Although these things are essential, they too often focus on what God can do for us, or what we can do for one another, rather than what we can do to glorify our Lord.

God "delights in the praises of His people" (Psalm 22:3) and is worthy of our "sacrifice of praise—the fruit of lips that confess His name" (Hebrews 13:15, NIV). Singing gives young people an opportunity to bless their Lord through words of adoration, thanksgiving, and praise. For these reasons, singing is an essential expression of worship that must not be overlooked in any youth ministry.

Finally, let's remember the positive impact and growth that will occur as your students begin to worship. I love a statement that Ken Poure, director at large for Hume Lake Christian Conference Center, once shared at our church: "God knew what He was doing when he commanded His people to worship Him. Not because He needs our worship, but because He knew what it would do for us."

THE CHALLENGE
"I know worship needs to be a more important part of my ministry, but trying to get teens to participate in meaningful singing is like trying to get them to wear polyester!" Believe me, I understand this frustration. I've heard all the complaints before:

• "Singing is boring. Why can't we do something else?"
• "I hate all these old songs; they're stupid."
• "I can't sing and I don't want to."
• "Sure, I'd sing, but I'd be the only one."
• "Singing is for girls . . . and wimps."
• "My youth pastor is a lame worship leader; he can't even tune his guitar."

These feelings are not hard for me to understand because when I was in high school, I voiced many of these complaints myself. The fact that my mom was the church choir director added to my rebellion! Like some students you'll encounter, I was the one who would rather have been playing capture the flag or watching a video. Praising God just didn't seem that important to me.

In addition to the complaints, the second challenge most youth workers will face is trying to get younger students, particularly junior highers and high-school underclassmen, to respond in worship. Although you might make singing and worship a regular practice at your youth meetings, that doesn't guarantee that young people will join in.

Studies in adolescent faith development reveal that teens in the seventh to ninth grades "are still concrete in their conceptions and egocentric in their relationships. God is perceived as an old man with white hair who is distant and not directly involved with their affairs."[5] This isn't to say that you can't stretch their understanding and teach them to worship, but such a perception of God is a challenge to overcome.

STEPS TO TAKE
Faced with the complaints and the immaturity of your students, you might be tempted to throw in the towel (or the guitar!), but wait. Here are some practical suggestions for making worship a top priority in your group—steps that will help you reach your students and overcome their apprehensions.

Step One: Frequency
In an article from *The Complete Book of Youth Ministry*, veteran songleader/writer Sonny Salsbury describes the importance of placing a priority on frequent youth singing. He relates this story: "I recently spoke for a week of chapel services at a large Christian junior high school. I prepared song sheets and started each day's service with some group singing. They started slow, but by the end of the week were really singing great. . . . The faculty informed me that they had done no singing in chapel for two years, but our week together convinced them that they should start again."[6]

In order for worship to make an impact in your ministry, it has to be done frequently. In our group we worship a minimum of twice a week.

If you establish a pattern of consistent worship, the results may surprise you, especially if you miss a time or two. Your students will be asking, "Hey, why didn't we get to worship tonight?"

Step Two: Time

I recently served for five years at a large church in southern California. One of the first things I noticed when I joined the staff was how bored and uninterested the students were with group singing. But they had reason to be.

Their previous efforts at worship consisted of three or four songs on Sunday morning, sometimes designed as much to quiet the students down as to worship God. Although there were many problems, the main difficulty was that our students were simply not being given enough time to enter into worship. Just as it often takes young people time to open up and relax in a small-group discussion or begin to share their prayer requests, it also takes time for them to respond in worship.

We began committing 20 to 30 minutes each Sunday and midweek for singing and worship. And you know what? It worked! Of course it didn't happen overnight, but today that group is known for having students who really love to worship God. This increased desire to praise the Lord has also contributed to a hunger within many of the students to learn more about Him and to serve Him more fully.

I recently spoke to the worship leader for a large youth group in southern California. He has experienced similar results by giving worship priority time in his youth group. In fact, one of their most well attended youth meetings is a Friday night (yes, Friday night in southern California!) worship-and-prayer meeting that runs for two hours.

Step Three: Quality

If worship is going to be a priority in your group, then it naturally follows that you need to make it worthwhile. This doesn't mean you have to have expensive sound equipment and professional-sounding singers and instruments; although, depending on your situation, these things can be valuable and may very well enhance the quality of your worship experience. But more importantly, the quality of your worship can be determined by the amount of preparation you make.

Quality times of singing and worship begin with preparation.

Think about how long you prepare to talk to students about God. How much more so should we prepare for a time when our students will be talking directly *to* God. With that in mind, it follows that the worship leader should practice and learn his or her material. Nothing ruins a worship time more than an unprepared leader who is fouling up the words or music to a song. (Effective preparation for worship will be addressed more completely in a later chapter.)

Step Four: Vertical Worship
When we speak of "horizontal" worship, we are talking about songs and words that tell us about God or the Christian life. It might also involve singing songs with comical lyrics and even crazier hand motions to one another! "Vertical worship," on the other hand, consists of songs that we sing directly to God. Of course there is a place for this first category of songs (and I use them regularly), but they are no substitute for the more powerful and intimate "vertical" songs that speak directly to God. These songs draw students directly into the presence of God as they turn your students' focus upward. But remember, both styles are important and have a place in your youth group. (We'll take a closer look at song selection later.)

PRIORITY PAYS OFF
Here's part of a letter that one of my former students wrote to me a few months after she left our group for college. It pleased me to hear the positive impact worship had on her life:

Dear Jim,

Can you believe my first semester at college is almost over? My classes have been *so* hard, but I have most of them with one of my roommates, so we've kind of gotten each other through it. . . . I've gotten involved with a small Bible study with some of the other Christians in the dorms. It's pretty good, but the singing really lacks. I really miss the worship at our church. I remember coming to Lifestyle [midweek Bible study] at times feeling really stressed out, but somehow I always felt uplifted after the worship. Boy, I could sure use that now!

I loved when we turned down the lights and sang. I could really feel the Holy Spirit. I guess I just appreciate it more now that I'm not there. Thanks, you really helped me learn how to worship, and it made a big difference in my spiritual life.

Love,
Tracy

Where is worship in your list of ministry priorities? In the middle? Near the bottom? Or perhaps it's one of those things you've been meaning to get around to? I encourage you to give worship its proper (and not to mention biblical) place. Not only will it bring honor to the Lord, but you will also begin to give your students a deeper desire to know, love and in turn, serve their Heavenly Father.

Let us then answer the challenge and example of Luther in our ministries by "knowing God through worship . . . responding with grateful songs of praise!"

THINK ABOUT IT

1. Where does worshipping God through singing fall in the order of your ministry priorities?

PRIORITY #1————————————————————————

PRIORITY #2————————————————————————

PRIORITY #3————————————————————————

PRIORITY #4————————————————————————

PRIORITY #5————————————————————————

2. Think about the quote by Richard Foster we read earlier in this chapter regarding the priority of worship:

    "The divine priority is worship first, service second. Our lives are to be punctuated with praise, thanksgiving and adoration. Service flows out of worship. Service as a substitute for worship is idolatry. Activity may become the enemy of adoration."

    What do you agree or disagree with in his statement?

3. Exercise: Take 15 minutes to thumb through the Psalms and record as many references to singing as you can find. Record them here for future reference.

    ————————————————————————————

    ————————————————————————————

    ————————————————————————————

    ————————————————————————————

4. Evaluation: On a scale of one (unenthusiastic) to 10 (very enthusiastic), how do your students respond to singing?

    1   2   3   4   5   6   7   8   9   10

2

BUILDING A BIBLICAL BASIS

To worship is to bow down before God, to give Him worth that is due Him. I feel like I am being laid at the feet of Jesus and my worries are taken away and given to Him. It is the relational part of my time with God.

Brad—12th grade

Worship makes me feel one with God. It reminds me of how awesome He is and how much I need Him. It gives me an opportunity to express to Him how I feel.

Michelle—10th grade

n researching the material for this chapter, I thought it would be interesting to visit a high school campus after school and ask several randomly selected students this question: What comes to mind when you think of the word worship? Some of the responses given included:

- "If you're really in love with your boyfriend or girlfriend, it's like you worship them."
- "It's what religious people do on Sundays."
- "Idolizing something or somebody."
- "Praising God."
- "Isn't it something Buddhist monks do in the mountains of China?"

Interesting responses indeed! Yet ask the same question to your youth group (or anyone in your church for that matter), and I'm sure you'll get a variety of responses, too. In fact, the subject of worship just might be one of the most controversial and misunderstood aspects of the church today.

Think about it; almost everyone has an opinion on the matter of worship, from the choir director to the church custodian. Some base their responses on feelings, some on tradition, and others on personal experience.

Consider the following definitions and thoughts on worship from these recognized authorities who have all written on this subject:

Worship is an active response to God whereby we declare His worth. Worship is not passive, but is participative. Worship is not simply a mood; it is a response. Worship is not just a feeling; it is a declaration.[1]

Ronald Allen and Gordon Borror

To worship is to quicken the conscience by the holiness of God, to feed the mind with the truth of God, to purge the imagination by the beauty of God, to devote the will to the purpose of God.[2]

William Temple

Our worship practices, like our relationship with the Lord, should reflect both majesty and intimacy.[3]

Don Wyrtzen

Worship is for God. He is our Creator, and the worship of his creatures is both his right and his pleasure. Worship is first and foremost for his benefit, not ours, though it is marvelous to discover that in giving him pleasure, we ourselves enter into what can become our richest and most wholesome experience in life.[4]

Graham Kendrick

Worship is human response to divine initiative.[5]

Richard Foster

Worship is the believer's response of all that he is—mind, emotion, will,

26

and body—to all that God is and says and does. This response has its mystical side in subjective experience, and its practical side in objective obedience to God's revealed truth. It is a loving response that is balanced by the fear of the Lord, and it is a deepening response as the believer comes to know God better.[6]

Warren Wiersbe

Worship connects me with the past, gives meaning to the present, and inspires hope for the future as my soul and spirit become blended again into the drama of Christ's life, death, and resurrection.[7]

Robert E. Webber

Christian worship establishes and expresses the personal character of the relations between God and humanity. The character of Christian worship is that of an encounter in which God speaks to us and gives us the tokens of his love, and in which we offer him our praise and thanks, seek his forgiveness and renew our commitment, ask his help and entrust our future to him.[8]

Geoffrey Wainwright

Christian worship is the adoration and service of God the Father through the mediation of the Son and prompted by the Holy Spirit.[9]

Ralph P. Martin

Worship is to feel in your heart and express in some appropriate manner a humbling but delightful sense of admiring awe and astonished wonder and overpowering love in the presence of that most ancient Mystery, that Majesty which philosophers call the First Cause, but which we call Our Father Which Art in Heaven.[10]

A. W. Tozer

These eloquent definitions written by godly men both teach and inspire me. Each one gives a different slant on an aspect of worship. Each one contains truth. Each one represents a personal understanding and experience based on study and spiritual reflection. What is your understanding of worship? Have you developed your own definition? Perhaps the best way to begin, so as to avoid confusion, is to go directly to the source—the biblical source that is. To establish an understanding of worship from its biblical perspective, remember that there are many aspects to the idea and practice of worship (as demonstrated by the definitions already given). For example, praise, thanksgiving, rejoicing, celebration, service, reverence, and humility are all involved in the total experience of biblical worship, and each of these can be reflected in worship through singing.

ORIGINS

The following is a brief survey of words associated with biblical worship. It is important to explore a word in its original language and context(s) in order to gain a clearer understanding of its historical usage and range of meaning. In addition, word studies typically reveal that there are several Hebrew and Greek words that have come to be represented by a single word in English.

My intent is not to provide an exhaustive analysis of the words presented, but to study the more common words associated with worship and praise in order to emphasize their relationship to singing. As worship leaders we have a responsibility, as teachers do, to be educated in the area we lead. On the practical side, I've also found that sharing a word's original meaning during a time of worship with students often adds to the quality of our time together and teaches them something in the process.

If you don't know Hebrew or Greek, don't worry. By using certain tools, namely, reference books that are user-friendly, anyone can get at a word's original meaning in the biblical languages. (For further study, I've included in the Resources section at the back of this book a list of additional works you may find helpful.)

Worship

Shacah (shaw-khaw) (Hebrew): "to prostrate oneself, to bow in homage, humbly beseech, do reverence."

Shacah is the most common Hebrew word translated "worship" in the Old Testament. While it can be expressed through singing, it is also understood as an act of prayer and as an acknowledgment of who God is: His attributes, person, and character.

O COME, let us sing for joy to
the Lord;
Let us shout joyfully to
the rock of our salvation.
Let us come before His
presence with thanksgiving;
Let us shout joyfully to
Him with psalms. . . .
Come, let us worship and
bow down;
Let us kneel before the
Lord our Maker. (Psalm 95:1-2, 6)

Exalt the Lord our God,
And worship at His footstool;
Holy is He. (Psalm 99:5)

So the people believed; and when they heard that the Lord was concerned about the sons of Israel and that He had seen their affliction,
then they bowed low and worshipped. (Exodus 4:31)

See also Genesis 22:5; 2 Samuel 12:20; and Isaiah 66:23.

Proskuneo (pros-koo-neh-o) (Greek): "to worship, do obedience,
prostrate oneself, do reverence."
The word *proskuneo* meant literally "to kiss towards" and conveyed
the picture of the worshipper bowing down and delivering a kiss (perhaps on the hand) to the one being worshipped. In the New
Testament, *proskuneo* is used exclusively for the worship of God or
Christ and is found 59 times, making it the most common word translated "worship." The thought behind the word suggests an inward attitude of humility and reverence typically expressed through prayer or
song as well as a beautiful picture of the adoring, intimate relationship
of God's children to the Father.[11]

Then Jesus said to him, "Begone, Satan! For it is written, 'You shall
worship the Lord your God, and serve Him only'." (Matthew 4:10)

God is spirit, and those who worship Him must worship in spirit and truth. (John 4:24)

And he said, "Lord, I believe." And he worshipped Him. (John 9:38)

And all the angels were standing around the throne and around the elders and the four living creatures; and they fell on their faces before the throne and worshipped God. (Revelation 7:11)

See also 1 Corinthians 14:25; Hebrews 1:6; Revelation 4:10; and 19:10.

Latreuo (lat-ryoo-o) (Greek): "to serve, to render religious service or homage, to worship."

This is an important word for describing worship because it reveals that worship is more than an act of reverence, praise, or adoration; it is also an expression of active service unto God. This expression can be inward as well as outward.

But this I admit to you, that according to the Way which they call a sect I do serve the God of our fathers, believing everything that is in accordance with the Law, and that is written in the Prophets. (Acts 24:14)

I urge you therefore, brethren, by the mercies of God, to present your bodies a living and holy sacrifice, acceptable to God, which is your spiritual service of worship. (Romans 12:1)

For we are the true circumcision, who worship in the Spirit of God and glory in Christ Jesus and put no confidence in the flesh. (Philippians 3:3)

See also Acts 7:42 and Hebrews 10:2.

As mentioned at the outset of this chapter, worship tends to mean different things to different people, including your students. Yet as we have seen through an examination of the words used in their original languages and contexts, worship is a multifaceted activity character-ized by both an inward attitude of the heart and an outward expression of response. Inwardly, a humble heart and reverent spirit recognize God for who He is, which leads to outward responses of praise, prayer, and service.

Young people must realize that worship is more than singing songs to God at youth group; it is an activity of devotion, empowered by the Holy Spirit, in recognition and thanksgiving for who God is.

Praise

Halal (haw-lal) (Hebrew): "to praise, boast about, to make a show of, celebrate."

The most frequent use of *halal* relates to praising God (hallelujah means "praise the Lord"). God is to be praised in all His fullness with an attitude of delight and rejoicing. Singing is the most common expression of praise and is an essential element in both public (Psalm 148) and private (Psalm 146:1-2) worship."[12]

And he [David] appointed some of the Levites as ministers before the ark of the Lord, even to celebrate and to thank and praise the Lord God of Israel: . . . with musical instruments, harps, lyres; also Asaph played loud-sounding cymbals. (1 Chronicles 16:4-5)

Moreover, King Hezekiah and the officials ordered the Levites to sing praises to the Lord with the words of David and Asaph the seer. So they sang praises with joy, and bowed down and worshipped. (2 Chronicles 29:30)

I will praise the name of God with song,
And shall magnify Him with thanksgiving. (Psalm 69:30)

My heart is steadfast, O God;
I will sing, I will sing praises, even with my soul. (Psalm 108:1)

Every day I will bless Thee,
And I will praise Thy name forever and ever.
Great is the Lord, and highly to be praised;

31

And His greatness is unsearchable. (Psalm 145:2-3)

See also Nehemiah 12:2; Psalm 22:26; 119:64; and Joel 2:26.

Yadah (yaw-dah) (Hebrew): "confession of sin" (Psalm 32:5); "declaration of God's attributes and works" (Psalm 138:2); "to give thanks in praise" (Nehemiah 12:46); "to praise God in song and with instruments" (Psalm 33:2).[13] This word comes from the Hebrew root word *yad* meaning "hand" and can also suggest praising God with extended hands.[14]

So it shall be when he becomes guilty in one of these, that he shall confess that in which he has sinned. (Leviticus 5:5)

And the heavens will praise Thy wonders, O Lord;
Thy faithfulness also in the assembly of the holy ones.
(Psalm 89:5)

Give thanks to the Lord of Lords,
For His lovingkindness is everlasting. (Psalm 136:3)
Give thanks to the Lord with the lyre;
Sing praises to Him with a harp of ten strings. (Psalm 33:2)

See also Psalm 32:5; 105:1-7; and 2 Chronicles 5:13.

Zamar (zaw-mar) (Hebrew): "to sing praise to God, make music in praise, celebrate through song and dancing."
While many of the other words translated "praise" can be used in differing contexts, *zamar* is strictly tied to praise through song and music. One of its parallel terms is the word used for the title of the book of Psalms, which literally means "praises."[15]

Sing praise to the Lord, you His godly ones,
And give thanks to His Holy name. (Psalm 30:4)

The Lord is my strength and song,
And He has become my salvation;

This is my God, and I will praise Him;
My father's God, and I will extol Him. (Exodus 15:2)

Sing to Him, sing praises to Him;
Speak of all His wonders. (Psalm 105:2)

Let them praise His name with dancing;
Let them sing praises to Him with timbrel and lyre.
(Psalm 149:3)

See also Psalm 7:17; 21:13, 66:4; and 146:2.

Aineo (ahee-neh-o) (Greek): "to praise."
The LXX (symbol for the Septuagint, the first Greek translation of the Hebrew Old Testament) uses *aineo* as the translation of *halal* and *yadah*. It is used to describe the reaction of angels (Luke 2:13) and men (Luke 2:20 and 19:37) who recognize God's glory and majesty. *Aineo* is also used to describe praise for God's actions (Acts 2:47 and 3:8-9).[16]

And suddenly there appeared with the angel a multitude of the heavenly host praising God, and saying, "Glory to God in the highest / And on earth peace among men with whom He is pleased." (Luke 2:13-14)

And as He was now approaching, near the descent of the Mount of Olives, the whole multitude of the disciples began to praise God joyfully with a loud voice for all the miracles which they had seen. (Luke 19:37)

See also Romans 15:11 and Revelation 19:5.

Eucharisteo (yoo-khar-is-tee-ah) (Greek): "to thank, to be thankful, giving of thanks."
In its classical usage, the root word *char* expresses the idea of a joyous feeling. It is where the Greek word for grace (*charis*) originates, and when combined with the prefix *eu* (well, rightly), the thought of gratitude or thankfulness is understood. In the New Testament,

eucharisteo is almost exclusively used for thanksgiving unto God and is commonly tied to the activity of praise and worship.[17]

> Let the word of Christ richly dwell within you, with all wisdom teaching and admonishing one another with psalms and hymns and spiritual songs, singing with thankfulness in your hearts to God. (Colossians 3:16)

> Devote yourselves to prayer, keeping alert in it with an attitude of thanksgiving. (Colossians 4:2)

> Amen, blessing and glory and wisdom and thanksgiving and honor and power and might, be to our God forever and ever. Amen. (Revelation 7:12)

See also Ephesians 1:16; Philippians 4:6; and 1 Thessalonians 5:18.

For the most part, the words associated with praise and worship indicate that it is a response of joy and thanksgiving (usually through song) directed to God in the acknowledgment of who He is and what He has done for His creation. Biblical praise is often accompanied by music, the lifting of hands, and even dancing. Praising God is expressive in nature and can be given both in a spirit of reverence or celebration.

Students cannot be forced to praise God with joy and celebration; it must come from within. The inclination of the frustrated though well-meaning youth worker might be to somehow manufacture a response of praise from his or her students that is not genuine. Such tactics will only backfire in the end. When young people begin to grow in their love for God they will become sensitive to His Spirit and responsive to His will for their lives—genuine worship and praise can be the only natural result.

WHY WORSHIP?
He Is Worthy
We worship and praise the Lord because He alone is worthy of our "sacrifice of praise" (Hebrews 13:15). Idols made of wood or stone were not worthy of worship in biblical times just as modern-day idols

are not worthy of a Christian's worship today. Teenagers might sing the praises of a new car, boyfriend or girlfriend, rock band, or celebrity, but these objects of value, though enjoyable, are not worthy of worship.

God alone, the Creator of all things (Colossians 1:16) is to be given our offering of worship. After all, when your mother makes a delicious meal, you don't say, "I thank thee fried chicken that thou art so tender, and moist potatoes that thou art so tasty." No! We thank the "creator," in other words . . . Mom! The worship of the good things in life (yes, even a new boyfriend or car) needs to go to the Lord, the Creator of all good things.

Psalm 18:3 declares, "I call upon the Lord, who is worthy to be praised." Not only is God worthy of our worship, but we are called to worship Him. The psalmist admonishes God's people to:

> Sing to the Lord a new song;
> Sing to the Lord, all the earth. . . .
> Ascribe to the Lord glory and strength.
> Ascribe to the Lord the glory of His name;
> Bring an offering, and come into His courts.
> Worship the Lord in holy attire;
> Tremble before Him, all the earth. (Psalm 96:1, 7-9)

To Glorify God

Another reason worship must be encouraged among our students is that it is an opportunity for them to give glory to God. The First Article of the Westminster Confession states that the chief end and duty of man is to glorify God and to enjoy Him forever.

Not only can students learn to enjoy God now through their worship times, but they can look forward to an eternity of being in the presence of God, giving Him glory. As the Apostle John received the Lord's Revelation, he was given a glimpse of heaven and noted that thousands upon thousands worshipped the exalted Christ and said with a loud voice, "Worthy is the Lamb that was slain to receive power and riches and wisdom and might and honor and glory and blessing" (Revelation 5:12).

Commenting on the activity of giving glory to God through worship,

C. S. Lewis insightfully exclaimed, "In commanding us to glorify Him, God is inviting us to enjoy Him."[18] Do your young people enjoy God through the times of worship in your group? If so, then I would imagine that at some point your group's worship times together ultimately focus directly on the Lord. If not, perhaps the emphasis of your worship times needs a little realigning. We'll get to that in the next chapter.

We Are Called As "Priests" to Worship

A final reason we worship God is because as "priests" we are called to worship Him. We are no longer under the Old Testament priestly system where the levitical priests made sacrifices for the sins of God's people. These priests also made intercession on behalf of the people unto God, and only the high priest could enter the holy of holies in the inner sanctum of the temple once a year to be in the direct presence of God. Yet with the sacrifice of God's ultimate High Priest, Jesus (Hebrews 7:26-27), the temple veil was torn in two (Matthew 27:51); thus enabling all who call upon the name of the Lord to come to Him directly (Hebrews 4:15-16).

As fellow priests in the body of Christ, we are called to "offer up spiritual sacrifices acceptable to God through Jesus Christ" (1 Peter 2:5). In his book *Worship Is a Verb*, Robert E. Webber notes the incorrect performer/audience mode that has crept into our present-day worship and calls for a "radical rediscovery of the principle of the priesthood of all believers—a principle that encourages everyone to become involved in a participating manner in offering the worship of praise and thanksgiving to the Father."[19] Therefore, since we are all members of the priesthood of believers (teenagers included), the importance of encouraging everyone in your group to participate in worship should be evident and a goal you should strive to meet.

I hope that you will take this information and exhortation to worship to heart. Use it to help educate your students about the biblical aspects of worship and our call to lift our praises up to God.

THINK ABOUT IT

1. In what ways has your concept of worship changed after examining the biblical origins of the words for worship?

2. Think of several ways you might be able to teach your students about praise and worship using the word studies provided in this chapter.

3. Do your students understand why they worship God through singing? How can you prevent them from feeling that singing is just an obligation they have to fulfill?

4. Refer to C. S. Lewis' comment in regard to enjoying God: "In commanding us to glorify Him, God is inviting us to enjoy Him." Then ask yourself: Are you personally able to truly enjoy God as you give Him glory and praise? What about your students?

3

PRACTICES: THE WAY YOU DO THE THINGS YOU DO

Worship makes me at peace and causes me to focus on the Lord. The upbeat songs make me happy and glad I came . . . they're fun.

Shaleah—12th grade

I have seen how to worship God and love Him. I love worshipping God through songs. It makes me feel closer to Him.

Janet—6th grade

I admit it. I'm the type of guy who likes to know *why* I'm doing something before I actually try to make it happen. Call me old-fashioned or cautious, but I need a little reason, a hint of purpose, a measure of control, or a plan of attack before I'm ready to go. Maybe you're like that, too. However, Mrs. Sarah Winchester, the heiress to the famous Winchester Rifle fortune, was not.

On a recent vacation, I visited what is now known as the "Winchester Mystery House," a colossal architectural testimony to a lack of planning. After the death of her husband and only child, the eccentric widow came to San Jose, California and bought an eight-room farm house. Mrs. Winchester was deeply superstitious and believed that she was directed by spirits to continually build onto her house in order to preserve her life.

The resulting mansion is a construction oddity—a rambling maze of rooms, stairs, and windows with little apparent purpose. The house includes stairs that lead to ceilings, fireplaces without chimneys, costly tiffany glass windows that open into walls, and doors that lead nowhere. One staircase has forty-five steps and nine turns and ascends only eight-and-a-half feet!

Talk about a building inspector's nightmare! Somehow I don't think the California state building codes would allow such a construction fiasco today, yet there are times when we all go about our youth ministries in much the same fashion. We develop elaborate plans for programs that go nowhere or lead important ministry opportunities by the seat of our pants, "hoping" that something spiritual might just happen.

This is particularly the case with our times of singing. Few of us really take time to evaluate the purpose, style, direction, or impact of our group singing. Here are a few of the worship "blunders" I've made; can you relate to any of them?

- "My lesson is only 20 minutes, so we'll just sing for a little while longer." (using worship as a meaningless time filler)
- "Well, we've got an awful lot to cover tonight, but I guess we can sing a couple of songs." (using worship as an obligatory preliminary exercise)
- "OK gang, let's follow up that rousing chorus of "Grin Again Gang" with "Ha-La-La-La!" (using only "fun" songs with little spiritual significance)
- "All right now, I want everyone to close their eyes and bow down as we sing, "Change My Heart, Oh God"... and we're going to keep singing it until you mean it! (emphasizing heavy, intense worship to the exclusion of singing more uplifting and even "lighter" songs)
- "Welcome to the high school group, freshmen.... There are a lot of new things to get used to, but of course you know all our songs!" (using the same songs and worship style for junior and senior high, not taking into account the developmental differences in the groups)
- "Johnny, never mind that Father Francisco never does this. Just get back in line for aisle-rolling practice." (pressuring students into worship practices and experiences that are not familiar to them or

practiced by your church)
- "Singing? . . . Oh, yeah, well, uh . . . I'm sure that we'll sing today in 'big' church." (not making the effort to do youth singing at all)

Do your worship times reflect a well thought-out purpose, both biblically and practically? If they do, great. But if you feel that it may be time to evaluate your practices and clarify your goals, then keep reading.

PRACTICES

I use the term *practices* to refer to the approach and, more importantly, the mindset we take in leading our students in worship. Our approach and mindset will ultimately determine what we *do*. Although this concept could potentially include many things, let's focus for now on the following:

- The subtle differences between a song leading and worship leading perspective

- Initiating change in your group from familiar to less familiar worship practices

- Designing worship that fits the worshipper

WORSHIP LEADING VERSUS SONG LEADING MENTALITY

Steve was great up front and could always be counted on to get kids singing enthusiastically. This guy had rhythm. Not only was he an excellent guitar player, but Steve had a great voice and a warm, friendly smile. With all these qualities, it was easy to see why young people followed him so easily during a time of singing. Crazy hand motions, clapping, girls' parts, guys' parts, up-front student participation; it was all there . . . yet unfortunately, there it usually stopped.

Students frequently said they really enjoyed Steve's song leading in our group, but I always sensed that there was something missing, that our students should be experiencing something more.

I also have a friend, Lee, who only knows how to lead youth singing with "heavy" praise and worship. All his students ever get are intense times of worship; no upbeat, fun, or celebration songs. There is no levity with Lee; he is a very intense person. That's fine, but perhaps not all of his students are ready for that same degree of intensity in worship, at least not all the time.

Chris led singing for teenagers in a church with a similar style and tradition as Steve's. Like Steve, Chris was a fine musician and had a beautiful voice. The groups Chris led enjoyed getting wild with Chris as they sang crazy, upbeat songs. But I noticed something different about the way Chris led; it was more than just a good ol' time of singing. Chris had the ability to direct a group's energy away from itself and focus it on the Lord.

After pulling the group together with several upbeat songs, Chris would change the tone of the set as he moved the group into praise and worship choruses. During this time, I often saw students closing their eyes, lifting their hands, while still others put their arms around each other in the bonds of Christian community. One thing was clear: Chris was not only a good song leader, he was an effective worship leader as well.

There was a time when, like Lee, I did only praise and worship choruses with teenagers. We would typically spend more than a half hour worshipping God, usually ending our times with the lights low, in a serious, intimate mood. Many students enjoyed our style of worship and said they always felt they had come into contact with God as they sang to Him. Yet there were those students, particularly the younger ones, who were uncomfortable with our worship and thought it was too serious. They wanted something a little less intense, a little more lighthearted.

As a result, I began opening our sessions with more fun, lighthearted songs that gave students a chance to just have a great time with one another. I learned that no matter how "spiritual" kids can get, they still enjoy the crazier side of life and songs that promote that.

As you read these "case studies," perhaps you see yourself as a Steve or a Lee or a Chris, to one degree or another. My purpose is not to advocate one leadership style over another, but to help you understand that, regardless of the songs you are using, it is the perspective and direction of the worship leader that will create the difference in the end.

Most of us would agree that song leading for its own sake is a valid endeavor. After all, to get a rowdy and distracted group of kids to sing together joyfully and unified in one purpose, can be an important foundation for the more spiritual elements of the meeting to follow. In fact, when put into the proper Christian context, crazy, upbeat songs can even provide a kind of "horizontal" worship as it draws your group together into the fellowship of our Lord.

However, what takes the worship leader *beyond* song leading is not just mellow, spiritual songs or dimmed lights, but his or her mindset, attitude, sensitivity and approach. As we discover in the Bible, worship is intended primarily for God's benefit (although we are blessed by it). When a worship leader goes beyond just singing songs to lead students in true "vertical," God-focused worship, the experience is deeper and, in my estimation, ultimately more valuable.

If a leader views youth singing as simply a time to have fun, a tool to calm down or fire up students, a good youth activity on the level of a game or skit, a preliminary exercise or warm-up, or a chance to show off his or her talents, then that is all the youth singing will ever accomplish. However, when a worship leader acknowledges the ability and potential for young people to praise the Lord in expressive, intimate, and meaningful ways, and grow in their communication with Him, then singing will become a means to that end.

This type of leadership demands a deliberate sensitivity on the part of the leader to allow the Holy Spirit to work not only through himself and the songs, but in the lives of the students as well.

I encourage you, like my friend Chris, to seek a balance in material and to focus on the ultimate purpose for our music ministries to youth.

FROM FAMILIAR TO UNFAMILIAR WORSHIP PRACTICES

Perhaps a more appropriate title for this section might be, "How to Change Your Group's Worship Practices without Losing Your Job." Why? Because I am about to identify a very common scenario that occurs when nonexpressive youth groups from nonexpressive churches feel the urge to become more expressive in their worship practices. Take the case of the First Fundamental Conservative Evangelical Bible Church, U.S.A. (a fictionalized name, of course).

MOVING BEYOND SONG LEADING TO WORSHIP LEADING: AN ANALYSIS

ASPECT	SONG LEADING	WORSHIP LEADING
TIME	shorter: usually 10-15 minutes in length	longer: usually 20-40 minutes in length
NUMBER OF SONGS	four to five on average	six to nine on average
FUNCTION	used as an "opener" for speaker, etc., or can be viewed as an essential part of the program itself	essential part of the program itself and viewed just as important as the message or lesson
PURPOSE	creates a fun and energetic environment, brings kids together, focuses groups attention	creates an outlet for genuine response in worship, builds community, draws individuals into contact with God
LYRICS	"silly" or comical lyrics, songs about life, relationships, etc., songs about God or the Christian life	songs directed to God, Christ, or the Holy Spirit, often in the first person
PHYSICAL EXPRESSION	crazy hand and body motions, up-front student participation, clapping, shouting, etc.	clapping, standing, kneeling, bowing, raising hands, closing eyes, or quiet reverence
LEADER'S MINDSET	singing for singing's sake, good "group" activity, fun, brings kids together, good preliminary exercise	singing as an expression of worship, a vehicle to move students into a focused time with the Lord

A gospel-preaching church that emphasizes evangelism and missions, FFCEBC is very traditional when it comes to its worship practices. A visitor would notice that the hymnbooks in the pews are well worn, and the finely tuned pipe organ boasts a full sound. Congregational singing is typically reserved, inexpressive, and unemotional. Yet, youth pastor Jack's high school group at FFCEBC is another story.

Jack's students enjoy singing and worshipping to the latest and hottest youth group songs and praise choruses. Jack even has a band that leads the group. His kids really love worshipping to a style of their own and even their parents seemed to approve . . . until things began to change.

It started when Jack attended a conference sponsored by a denomination different from his own. He immediately noticed that during the worship sessions people felt free and uninhibited to show outward expression to the Lord. Some knelt, others raised their hands, and still others bowed down. Jack was moved by what he saw and was soon participating himself.

As soon as Jack returned to his youth group, he told his students that it was all right to show emotion and be expressive during worship (the Bible even mentions it!). He then strongly encouraged everyone in his group to raise their hands as they sang and worshipped that evening. Some students awkwardly tried to comply, others folded their arms in defiance, some laughed, and some just stood there looking totally confused. Within a week, youth pastor Jack found himself sitting before a group of concerned parents and a suspicious board of elders. To rephrase a popular children's rhyme:

Jack be foolish, Jack be blind
Jack jump over the acceptability line!

A BETTER WAY

Jack's unfortunate experience is not an uncommon one among youth leaders. His desire for change was not necessarily wrong, but he could have avoided his impending disaster had he been more careful in his approach to initiate change. The following is a list of things to consider and actions to take or not to take when attempting to change your youth group's worship practices.

Be Discerning

Discernment involves knowledge, understanding, and critical thinking. First, it is crucial that a youth worker seeking change in his or her group's worship should be aware of the worship practices of his or her congregation. While the majority of churches do not require their youth groups to adopt the same style of worship as the adult service, certain practices (many times involving outward expression) may not be considered appropriate.

Also, it is important to come to an understanding of what may or may not be acceptable in a given situation. In some circumstances you may find that your church leaders may grant you permission to experiment with more expressive styles of worship in the youth group setting; others may not. In any case, trying to initiate change without discernment or counsel from church leadership will almost certainly lead to conflict.

Although your new worship practices may be biblical and, in your thinking, harmless, it is not worth creating a rift in the church or animosity between the youth and the leadership. Remember, regardless of your particular feelings, your students and their families likely attend your particular church because they are comfortable with the leadership and worship style. Of course there is room for change or growth, but it should always be tempered with sensitivity and consideration for the church.

Be Sensitive

Because most people are somewhat cautious about change, it is wise to be as sensitive as possible to your students, their parents, and the congregation as a whole. Asking students to experiment with unfamiliar worship practices may make them feel uncomfortable and self-conscious to the point where they cannot worship at all. Also, keep in mind that it is difficult to take young people beyond the experiences of their parents and the church. On one occasion I had a group of students from a very conservative church kneel for prayer and worship. One of the students went home excited and told his mother about it. She called me the next day wanting to know what type of weirdness was going on in the youth group.

Many times such conflicts arise not because of weirdness, but because of worldview. A worldview is a set of assumptions based on personal and cultural experience that determines how we perceive our world, behave, and treat others. Worldviews may differ not only from culture to culture, but from generation to generation, and even from religion to religion. For example, Dr. Charles Kraft from Fuller Theological Seminary notes his own worldview and its difficulty with expressive worship when he states:

> As an American of my generation, raised in traditional white, middle-class evangelical churches, I have been carefully taught two important worldview values: 1) emotion is bad and 2) change, though acceptable in nearly every other area of life, is suspect in religion.[1]

Dr. Kraft represents the generation of the 40s and 50s, yet he realizes that his worldview is not better, just different. He suggests that today's youth are more open to change and encourages young people to explore unfamiliar territory with various worship practices. Relying on some good-natured sarcasm, he declares, "Some of our young people don't seem to have been taught (as I was) that when we read the Scriptures, we're suppose to ignore the passages where we are told to lift our hands (Psalm 134:2) or to dance (Psalm 149:3) or to praise God loudly (Psalm 150). . . . And they have often missed the message that it's not OK to change religion. So they do these things in church."[2]

As a leader, be sensitive and allow time for change to take place. Sometimes we tend to put our plans and egos ahead of the needs of our students. Remember, some may not be as ready for change as you are. For others, change may not occur at all, and that can be OK. Others will welcome change and hopefully grow closer in their walk with the Lord because they experience more meaningful times of worship.

A FINAL WORD

If the Lord has been leading you to consider challenging your students in some of the areas mentioned above, and your church is supportive, then rejoice! You may see worship enrich, encourage, and challenge your students . . . perhaps your whole church (I've seen it happen!). However, if you sense there may be some questions or conflicts, don't rush into things. First, try to discuss your feelings and reasons for wanting to implement change with your church's music minister or senior pastor. You may be surprised at their responses. If you come to the point where you feel convicted to worship using practices unfamiliar or contrary to your present church setting, then perhaps it's the Lord's way of prompting you to consider a change of ministry. Pray what the Lord would have you do, and seek His will and good pleasure in all things.

The Lord doesn't want you to be frustrated in ministry. At the same time, I doubt that He wants you to be the cause of division in your church, either.

WORSHIP THAT FITS THE WORSHIPPER

A common complaint many youth workers hear from their students is that the singing in the adult worship service is dull, boring, and difficult to relate to. As one of my more vocal students exclaimed to me once, "The hymns are usually slow and kind of 'marchy' and have words I can't understand or have never even heard of. Not only that, but the only other time I ever hear an organ played is at baseball games! At least I like 'Take Me Out to the Ballgame.'"

It's easy for many of us to see the gap between adult and teenage worship. What works for one group will not automatically work for another. While the differences in age and developmental maturity are obvious between teenagers and adults, the differences between junior highers and senior highers are just as important to consider. To reduce frustration and enhance the success of your worship ministry, take a look at your worship practices to see how well they match up with adolescent faith development.

Junior High Worship

I recommend Wayne Rice's *Junior High Ministry* for a complete treatment of the developmental stages junior highers experience in their world. In general, junior highers can be characterized in this way:

- *Physically*—they feel awkward, with many changes taking place that may embarrass them; they are also very energetic (as any junior high worker will tell you).
- *Socially*—they're self-conscious and unsure about their own identity; their need for peer recognition and belonging is very important.
- *Mentally*—they are moving from concrete to more conceptual thought processes, which can be both idealistic and judgmental.
- *Emotionally*—they're unpredictable and often intense; usually react ing to all the other developmental changes going on in their lives.
- *Spiritually*—they're interested in a practical emphasis of Christianity; they are also sensitive to sin and are beginning the process of faith ownership.

With this in mind then, what should junior high worship look like? Here's what Christian education specialist and teacher John Dettoni suggests:

> "Junior high worship is most effective when it is informal, life-related, fast-paced, and full of variety. Junior highers will not tolerate boredom or irrelevancy. They need to feel God's presence with them as they worship him and recognize that he is involved in their lives daily."[3]

In practical terms, be loose and casual when leading junior highers in singing. For example, instead of always having your song list prepared, ask your kids for their requests. My junior highers love to choose songs they want to sing, and it adds to their self-confidence as well. Second, because their attention span is still short, keep your worship times short (10 to 15 minutes); or break up the singing into several sets during a meeting. For example, you may start a meeting with 10 to 15 minutes of "rowdy" songs and close it with several praise choruses.

Third, remember that junior highers are typically energetic, so don't hesitate to sing songs that require a lot of hand motions, audience participation, and volume! I also suggest selecting songs that teach practical Christianity—songs dealing with obedience, sin, relationships, God's love, faithfulness, and forgiveness to name a few. I've also found junior highers to be very responsive to short times of teaching on a song's meaning before singing it; this can help give them a focus while singing. Take advantage of spiritual insights during times of singing and worship, and allow for student response. In other words, be attentive to the mood of your students.

In relation to "spirituality," be sensitive to the awkwardness that many of your junior highers are experiencing. Intimate reflection and outward spiritual expression may be more than many can handle; you may want to save such emphasis for senior high students.

High School Worship

To understand the developmental stages of high school students and how to minister to them, I recommend the book *High School Ministry* by Mike Yaconelli and Jim Burns. The general developmental characteristics typical of high school students include:

- *Physically*—they are still self-conscious about appearance, yet developing self-confidence steadily; typically, they're not as energetic as junior high students, but are able to focus and concentrate longer.
- *Socially*—they are learning to experience and develop individuality, yet they're still dependent upon the peer group for support and acceptance. Their relationships, which they take seriously, are often the means by which many adolescents identify themselves.
- *Mentally*—they are able to think in more abstract ways; they are also reflective, introspective, and idealistic, yet they can be suspicious and questioning.
- *Emotionally*—they can be up one minute and down the next (mood swings are quite typical of this age group); they tend to be self-centered yet are moving towards an others-centered mindset.
- *Spiritually*—they seek faith ownership; to them, the practical and relational emphases of Christianity are important; they are aware of inconsistent and exemplary models within Christianity and can be affected by both. They can experience a period of growing commitment or falling away, where questioning and reflective thought concerning God and the Christian life can determine their involvement.

What then should we consider when leading senior highers in

singing and worship? First, while senior highers enjoy fast-paced songs with a lot of energy, full sound, and movement, they also enjoy quieter times of worship. High school students have the ability to appreciate songs with deeper lyrical content. For this reason, you may wish to focus on themes such as humility, God's sovereignty, spiritual warfare, and so on.

Because high school students have a longer attention span, you may want to experiment with your time allowance for singing and worship. As mentioned earlier in this chapter, it takes time for high schoolers to open up in worship. Twenty to 30 minutes seems to be adequate in most cases for students to enter into meaningful worship.

Senior highers are also influenced by their emotions. While some worship leaders neglect teenage emotions altogether, others use emotion as a subtle form of manipulation to get students to react. Both extremes should be avoided. Instead, encourage students to express themselves in appropriate ways during times of singing and worship. The worship of God needs to be experienced by your young people not only intellectually but emotionally as well.

Finally, allow your times of singing to be community builders for your senior highers. As they experience closeness to God through singing His praises, they will, in turn, be compelled to exhibit that same closeness towards one another.

THINK ABOUT IT

1. After reading this chapter, how would you generally describe your leadership?
   A) song leader   B) worship leader   C) balance of both

2. If you tend to be a song leader exclusively, what are some mental, spiritual and attitudinal changes you could start working on that would help you better lead your students in worship?

   Mental: _____
   Spiritual: _____
   Attitudinal: _____

3. When have you tried to introduce unfamiliar worship practices to your students? What was the result? If you haven't, what changes would you like to implement, and how do you think your students and your church leadership would respond?

4. Is your worship for junior highers the same in content and style as your high school worship? If so, what changes could you implement to make it more appropriate for each group?

4

THOSE WHO LEAD: QUALITIES TO CONSIDER AND DEVELOP

Worship makes me feel good inside. When I'm depressed at any time, I know that when we have worship I feel so much better and all my problems go away when I sing to Him. I feel like He can hear my prayer to Him. He gives me a sense of relief and everything is fine. He wants me to know that He cares and that I need to give everything to Him.

Tina—12th grade

Worship is a time when I feel the closest to the Lord. I think music is a special way of communicating with God.

Jennifer—11th grade

f you're concerned about providing your students with a quality song and worship ministry, you'll need to start by putting a quality person in the key leadership role. Just as there are certain qualities a pastoral search team will consider in selecting a senior pastor, there are also qualities to look for in a youth worship leader. A fellow youth pastor friend of mine learned this the hard way.

Ted was the youth pastor at a small church and found himself in need of a worship leader for his group of 20 students. Enter Phil, the only guitar player in the church. Ted rigorously recruited Phil to lead worship for the teenagers, but it was clear almost from the start that Ted's new worship leader was unqualified. Sure, Phil could play guitar and sing—and he did both quite well—but Phil's weaknesses far outweighed his musical abilities.

Although Phil was willing to lead, he was not involved in personal worship. He did not spend any significant time in prayer or in the Word, and until he was recruited to help with the youth, his attendance was even sporadic. Several people in the church had commented positively to Ted that "an opportunity like this may be just what Phil needs to get more involved." But while Phil was growing slowly in his Christian life, he was really not to the point of leading others in spiritual matters—especially worship. Finally, Phil's style of worship leading was more characteristic of a performer than a ministry facilitator. He came, played, and left, leaving the students with a what-just-happened feeling.

While Phil's case was extreme, it was not fatal. In fact, he eventually came back as a worship leader for that group several years later, after his spiritual walk and ministry skills had matured.

Here are some qualities to look for in the person who has the *primary* responsibility of worship leading for your group.

SPIRITUAL QUALITIES
Since leading worship is a spiritual ministry then it follows that certain spiritual qualities should be evident in the lives of those who lead. Whether you, a volunteer, or perhaps even a student leads the worship for your group, effective ministry can only ultimately be achieved when those leading are walking with the Lord.

1. Giftedness
Romans 12:6-8, 1 Corinthians 12:8-10, Ephesians 4:11, and 1 Peter 4:11 all discuss the topic of spiritual gifts. What your particular tradition believes about these gifts is not my concern. The point is that the church of individuals gifted for various aspects of ministry for "the common good" (1 Corinthians 12:7) and "the equipping of the saints for the work of service, to the building up of the body of Christ" (Ephesians 4:12).

Certain individuals may have a heart for worship but may not be spiritually gifted for *leading* worship. Still, you may ask, "Where in Scripture is the spiritual gift of worship leading mentioned?" The answer may be that the spiritual qualities necessary for a worship leader are characterized by the qualities listed for other ministries of service within the church. For example, to effectively lead a group of students in worship, a person must have a desire to see spiritual growth in those he or she leads. It is a kind of *pastoral* gift that God bestows on leaders. One could say that the worship leader shepherds his flock in the area of worship (Ephesians 4:11).

The spiritual gift of *service* or ministry mentioned in Romans 12:7 may also be appropriate for those who minister in worship leading. Also, Romans 12:8 lists the gift of *leadership* as a ministry within the body of Christ. Do not those who stand before a congregation and invoke worship lead? You may wish to study these three gifts in more depth to gain a clearer and more personal understanding of your gifts as related to the position of worship leader.

2. Private Worshipper

Graham Kendrick is one of Great Britain's leading singer/songwriters and has led worship for many years, both with large and small groups. Speaking on the importance of personal worship, Kendrick admonishes worship leaders:

> To lead others in worship, you must be a worshipper. There is much truth in the saying that "you cannot take anyone further than you have been yourself," and if you do not have a real desire to worship God, you will not take others very far—in fact, they will probably overtake you! In the midst of all the practical considerations of choosing songs, sensing the atmosphere, playing the right chords, and so on, the over-riding activity must be to stir up your own spirit towards God and give him genuine thanks, love, and praise.[1]

The concept of "being" before "doing" is one of which we must constantly remind ourselves in youth ministry. Ours is typically a profession of producing . . . numbers, Bible studies, programs, ministries, etc. Yet without taking the time to get to know our Heavenly Father personally, to what does it all avail?

Private worshippers spend time in prayer and in God's Word. In commenting on this, Pastor Jack Hayford notes, "Before I attend to technical matters, I've learned to attend to spiritual concerns."[2] Spending daily time in God's Word and in prayer is the only source from which any of us, in particular the worship leader, can *receive* from the Lord; when we lead, we'll have something to *give* to others.

I've noticed personally that worship times are "flat" and even lifeless when I haven't been spending personal time with the Lord. On the other hand, some of our most meaningful times have occurred when I know I've been in close contact with the Lord and am allowing Him to work freely in my own life.

3. Fruitless or Fruitful?

Third, the worship leader should be manifesting the fruits of the Spirit to some degree in his or her life. Galatians 5:22-23 lists the spiritual qualities evident in a believer's life who is growing in the Lord: "But the fruit of the Spirit is love, joy, peace, patience, kindness, goodness, faithfulness, gentleness, self-control; against such things there is no law."

In other words, if someone is impatient, rude, self-centered, given to excesses, and so on, he is, in a sense, unspiritual and has no business leading worship. (It doesn't necessarily mean, however, that this person is unregenerate.)

Young people can spot a phoney a mile away. Those in any leadership role with teenagers must not only live lives according to the Spirit, but must walk in the Spirit as well (Galatians 5:25).

LEADERSHIP QUALITIES

It is also important to seek certain qualities of leadership and ability when choosing a worship leader. When combined with the spiritual qualities mentioned above, a solid worship ministry for your students should be the natural result. In other circumstances you may need to develop these qualities in those who are learning.

1. Self-Confidence

A degree of self-confidence is typically required of those in leadership positions in almost any facet of life. When I speak of self-confidence, I'm not talking about being all-knowing and all-powerful, or even an outgoing loudmouth type.

Because young people can be intimidating (have you ever stepped foot on an unfamiliar high school campus?), it is crucial that youth worship leaders possess and communicate a humble yet confident attitude of self-assurance. In other words, be yourself without compromise as you lead others in singing and worship. God has given each Christian certain personality traits, gifts, and abilities to be used in His service. In addition, there are certain limitations we all have too, whether technical, musical, or vocal. Self-confidence comes from knowing what those limitations are and accepting them. Tragically, I've seen many worship leaders who try to be something they're not in hopes of getting a better response out of the groups they lead.

Some try to be "Mr. Funny," "Mr. Cool," "Mr. Musician," or "Mr. Introspective," when they are really not that way at all. Remember: your mannerisms will always find you out! If you try to be something you're not in front of a group for whatever reason, your body language is bound to show it through nervousness, insincerity, awkwardness, or some other type of weakness.

So relax! When you're comfortable with yourself in a visible position of leadership, then those you lead will feel comfortable, too.

I remember my first youth ministry. I had a group of very patient high school kids who were the unfortunate "guinea pigs" for a youth leader who was just learning how to play guitar and lead worship. I was self-conscious of my mistakes and would often stop and apologize right in the middle of a song after missing a chord or striking the wrong note. The kids would usually just laugh and forgive me; they knew I was trying my best. I think they hung in there with me because I was myself with them and truly cared that they learned to worship God.

Their support really helped me build my own self-confidence, and their loving sense of humor helped us all learn together. When I wanted to teach them a new song, I'd ask them, "Hey, do you guys know this one?" They would respond, "Jim, if you can *play* it, we can *sing* it!"

2. Facilitator or Performer?
In my experience, effective song and worship leaders perform less and facilitate more. Yohann Anderson, a recognized authority on the

subject of youth song leading, agrees. He says:

> If you see yourself only in a performance mode, then you won't be a very good song leader. . . . [Facilitators] are constantly aware of the participation of the people around them. . . . You have to want to relate or it won't work. . . . The song leader's job is to help create an atmosphere for singing to naturally happen."[3]

One time I put together a praise band for a series of high-energy youth outreaches. Our group was complete with drums, bass, lead guitar, rhythm guitar, and keyboards. Not only that, but each one of the instrumentalists (except for yours truly) was a very talented musician. After a couple of practices I could tell that it was going to be a challenge to develop an effective blend because these guys all wanted their solo and moment of glory.

When the time came for us to lead singing, the kids who came to the outreaches loved the group. There was a lot of energy and the band cranked! However, later, when I asked several of the students and their adult leaders what they thought, their replies were virtually the same—they said they enjoyed the band, but the event was more like a concert than a time of singing and worship. We had definitely performed more than we had facilitated.

This isn't to say, of course, that an exellent musical artist or performer can't be a good worship leader. In fact, their technical expertise may free them up to be a very good facilitator. However in worship, the focus must be on leading your group, not on performing for them.

There are several differences between performance and a facilitating style of leadership for singing and worship. Consider the comparison below:

PERFORMER	FACILITATOR
• draws attention to himself	• draws attention to the Lord
• distracts with voice or unnecessary instrumentation	• concerned with keeping strong rhythm and blending
• interferes and interrupts flow in various ways	• prompts others to be involved and seldom breaks flow

• immersed in personal abilities	• allows God to use what abilities are available
• brings glory to self	• brings glory to God
• one-man-show mentality	• wants to encourage other musicians and students to glorify God with their gifts

After reading a list like this, which category best represents your leadership style or the style of your worship leader—performer or facilitator? Perhaps there are certain areas you can begin working on to improve your ability to facilitate group singing. (I'll deal with more specific ways to do this later.)

3. Musical and Technical Ability

Worship leading is 90 percent leadership and 10 percent musical or technical ability. You certainly don't need to be an excellent musician to be an excellent worship leader. In fact, I've known some great musicians who *weren't* good worship leaders because they were too hung up on musical perfection to focus on worship.

However, this doesn't negate the importance of musical ability. Far from it. The person who is the primary worship leader in your group (as opposed to backup musicians or vocalists) must have a voice that can project and enunciate properly. If playing a lead instrument (say guitar or piano), he or she should be able to keep good rhythm and represent the song accurately.

Believe it or not I've encountered individuals who had the 90 percent leadership part of worship leading covered but had to settle for mediocre worship because they simply did not have the musical or technical ability to make it happen.

Again, not everyone is gifted to lead worship. In fact, while I believe that everyone is musical to a degree, not everyone is cut out to play an instrument or sing in such a way that others can follow. Therefore, look for basic musical ability in those you choose to lead worship for your students and encourage them to practice and improve.

Psalm 33:3 encourages worship leaders to "sing to Him a new song / Play skillfully with a shout of joy." Just because it's youth worship does not mean that quality should be sacrificed. When we worship

59

God, we need to give Him our best.

In conclusion, I'm sure some of you are saying, "If I looked for every qualification you mentioned, I would eliminate all my possible worship leaders—including me!" I understand that most churches have limited resources and that most volunteers come to you as a sort of "diamond in the rough." Although you should identify the important spiritual qualities to seek in a worship leader, be willing and patient to teach, disciple, and train yourself or those interested in worship leading.

DISCIPLING OTHERS TO LEAD

Equipping others for the work of ministry is a foundational principle regarding the life and work of the church. For example, Paul encouraged his disciple Timothy to train others to teach. Second Timothy 2:2 says, "And the things which you have heard from me in the presence of many witnesses, these entrust to faithful men, who will be able to teach also."

Although worship leading is not specifically mentioned in this passage, I believe the principle of discipling can be understood to include a number of spiritual ministries. Are you presently enabling and training students to lead worship in your youth ministry?

Encourage Interested Students

Constantly be on the lookout for students or volunteer leaders who might be interested in song and worship leading. How can you discover them? Well, if you have one or two people constantly "hanging around" each week when you're preparing music or tuning your instrument, or who run up afterward to start playing with your guitar, chances are they're interested! Over the years I've noticed students picking up my guitar after a meeting and picking out the intro to "Stairway to Heaven" (inevitably the only thing they know on guitar). I usually approach them by saying something like, "I didn't know that was a Christian song." To which any typically sarcastic high school student would reply, "Well, it talks about heaven, doesn't it?"

Kids need to be encouraged. They might be intimidated to approach you about participating in worship leading because they feel they lack talent, don't have a knowledge of "praise" material, or feel afraid of getting up in front of their peers. It's up to you to make the first move! I like to set up appointments with students or leaders, either at the church or at their homes, to hear them play and to teach them some of the youth group songs. I've noticed that students respond well to this type of one-on-one encouragement.

While sharing songs together, remember to carefully weave in your philosophy of worship, so as to teach not only the material but the message *behind* the material. Teach them the *how*, the *who*, the *why*, and the *what* of worship. Finally, remember to encourage your students to be active in personal devotion and worship before attempting to lead others. While all this can be done individually with students, you may also wish to start a musicians' fellowship that meets once a week to train larger groups. Tell interested individuals to bring their instruments, Bibles, and note pads for learning new material, and inform them to be prepared for instruction and personal growth. I've known several groups who have developed similar fellowship groups with much success.

Provide Opportunities

Training must be followed with opportunities for active learning. This means giving your W.L.I.T. (worship leaders in training) experimental opportunities where they can learn from a qualified leader, then learn from their mistakes. I suggest following the tried-and-tested model for discipleship training that goes something like this:

"I lead . . . you watch."
"I lead . . . you assist."
"You lead . . . I assist."
"You lead . . . I watch."

For example, Juan was interested in leading worship, so I began working with him. He began by simply observing my style of worship leadership at our youth meetings, camps, and so on. I would often ask him what he observed, and we would discuss various aspects of song selection, group dynamics, musicianship, and so on. After practicing for several months, I asked Juan to assist me in leading worship. I remember introducing Juan to the group as my "new assistant," and he promptly received a round of rousing applause from his peers (they were pulling for him!).

Juan did a great job assisting me (he was an excellent guitar player), but he needed work on projecting his voice in order to lead vocally. The next step was encouraging Juan to take the primary role of vocal and instrumental leadership. Juan met the challenge and continued to work on his worship-leading abilities. I was right at his side, assisting him vocally and instrumentally, but it was Juan who was leading.

I've long since left that particular ministry, but do you know who is the worship leader for that group today, and who has trained numerous other students in worship leading? You guessed it—Juan!

If you also have enough interested individuals, you might want to start a worship team. This will give a greater number of students opportunities to participate and use their gifts for God's glory. Whether vocalist, bass guitar, acoustic or electric guitar, keyboard, drums, or horns, seek to create and provide opportunities for your students to get involved!

By making a commitment to discipling students in worship leading, you will naturally create student *ownership* of the worship ministry in your group. Participation will increase as a result because students will feel the singing time is theirs. I remember one time when some students were talking obnoxiously during a worship time and were quieted by their peers who wanted to worship. Talk about positive peer pressure!

Ministry Multiplied

Finally, realize that when you take the time to disciple others in an aspect of ministry that multiplication will usually result. By far the most satisfying aspect of my work with young people is hearing about those who, after they have graduated, go on to minister on their own in various places and in various ministries. Having students that you have discipled go on to lead worship on their college campuses, at youth camps, in ministries, or on the mission field are the sweet fruits of your music ministry.

THINK ABOUT IT

1. If you had someone leading your students in worship whom you later found out was spiritually unqualified, what would you do?

    A) Let him continue until you could find a replacement.
    B) Immediately terminate his ministry.
    C) Try to work with him on his spiritual weaknesses, while continuing to allow him to lead.

2. Spiritual giftedness, personal devotion to the Lord, and the fruits of the Spirit were mentioned as key spiritual ingredients to develop and look for in worship leaders. Do you agree with these qualifications? What would you add? Subtract?

3. If you're more performance-oriented, what are three things you could work on to become more of a facilitator?

    _____
    _____
    _____
    _____

4. What training and opportunities do you provide for individuals who are interested in song and worship leading? If nothing, where could you begin?

PART 2

TOOLS, TIPS, AND TECHNIQUES FOR EFFECTIVE SONG AND WORSHIP LEADING

T
he first section of this book was designed to address the *why* and *what* of song and worship leading with youth. The remaining chapters of this book are meant to give you the *how to's*. While volumes of how-to books on games, retreats, and meeting plans have been written for youth workers, there is very little on the subject of singing and worship.

The chapters that follow are the result of many years of trial and error, creativity, experimentation, and innovation. Some of the ideas are quite basic, but others will challenge and stimulate you to go beyond what you're already doing. I have tried to provide something for everyone, from the first time beginner to the veteran song leader. For example, if you are concerned you won't be able to develop an effective worship ministry because you don't play an instrument, fear not! There are several ways you can get around that obstacle. Or perhaps you are ready to start a praise band but are not quite sure where to begin. Read on! Or maybe your students just won't sing, and you're ready to throw in the towel. Wait! There are creative ways to get them to sing . . . and even to enjoy it!

We will also touch on practical issues, such as learning to make your own worship slides, writing songs, obtaining copyright permissions, and learning how to create different moods for meaningful worship.

Use what you need and save some ideas for later. But most of all, be sure to try something new. I promise that with some persistence, these worship ideas will reap great benefits for both you and your students.

5

FROM TAPE DECK TO PRAISE BAND

Worshipping Jesus makes my relationship better with Him. I love to sing to Jesus. Sometimes it makes me cry because He means so much to me and has done so much for me.

Shannon—10th grade

Worship makes me feel proud and happy and I think it makes Him happy too. I would feel pretty bad if I did not praise Him

Danny—6th grade

Y ou may be in a situation where you would like to see your students worshipping to a praise band, but you're not quite sure how to go about it. Or maybe you've tried a band and found that it was more hassle, more work, and more distraction than it was worth. Perhaps a small ensemble is working well in your situation (a couple of guitars, or maybe a guitar and keyboard), but you'd like to get creative with it and possibly add other instruments. Maybe there is no one to lead worship for your group, and you're in need of some viable alternatives.

Whatever your situation, this chapter will benefit you. I've led singing and worship using a variety of arrangements, and I am confident that there is an ideal setup for your group. It's also exciting to grow and expand your worship ministry to increase opportunities for students and volunteer leaders to use their gifts and talents for the Lord.

SINGING WITHOUT INSTRUMENTS

Jim, a friend of mine, was a youth worker who had a very successful high school program despite a challenging location: Hollywood. I asked Jim what he was offering his students, and he quickly rattled off a number of items including midweek Bible studies, games, skits, after–school weightlifting, service trips, retreats, campus outreach, and so on.

I asked him if his group ever sang. Jim responded, "Believe it or not, we hardly sing at all. There's just no one willing to lead our students in worship." I said, "Come on, Jim, you mean to tell me in a youth program like yours there's absolutely no one with the talents and willingness to lead music for your group?" Again he answered, "No. And that's why we don't sing in my youth group."

Perhaps your situation is similar to Jim's. Sometimes it's a real challenge trying to find someone qualified and willing to lead your students in worship. I encourage you not to give up but to consider some other options that may work well instead of, or until you locate, a worship leader.

Sing A Cappella

Singing a cappella means to sing without instrumental accompaniment. At first you might think this sounds like a rather boring or even intimidating suggestion (students might actually hear their own voices and be heard by others), but singing and worshipping in this manner can be very effective and rewarding.

With upbeat songs, establish rhythmic clapping to complement the singing. You can set a good strong rhythm by taking the time to get your students in sync with the beat of the song. Don't just say, "OK everybody, let's all clap along!" Instead, lead them in the clapping until a good, solid beat and rhythm is established, then add the words or hand motions.

Singing without instruments can also be very effective for quieter times of worship and praise. One time when I was in Mexico on a service weekend with my students, I came down with a terrible cold and literally could not hear to tune my guitar. Horror of horrors! I told the students that we couldn't worship around the campfire that night because I was unable to properly tune my God-given instrument for worship leading.

The kids were undaunted. They simply said, "Well then, we'll just have to worship without a guitar tonight." And you know what? We did. It was one of the most beautiful times of worship I've ever experienced with teenagers! God will be praised whether you sing a cappella or with a five-piece band.

Remember Paul and Silas singing praises to God during their imprisonment in a Philippian jail (Acts 16:25)? They wouldn't have dreamed of not worshipping God simply because they had no instrumental accompaniment. Who knows? Maybe they rattled their chains a bit!

One idea you can try is to turn the lights down low and have your students sit in a circle and sing a cappella in conjunction with a prayer-and-share time. I've had students tell me they enjoy hearing the group sing without instruments for a change. It creates a very intimate mood, which can be wonderful for a worship time.

Split-Track Recordings

Another option for singing and worship is to have your group use split-track recordings. Split-track recordings usually come in cassettes and are designed with separate vocal and instrumental tracks so that groups can listen to and learn the songs, then turn down the vocal track and sing along with the instruments only. All you need is a cassette player or stereo with a balance-control knob. Turning the balance-control knob one way or the other adjusts the relative volume of the vocal or instrumental track.

Several youth and music companies provide split-track recordings. You can obtain material ranging from "Pharaoh, Pharaoh" to "I Love You, Lord." These background tapes can be very effective with high-energy singing, clapping, and hand motions, but they work just as well during quieter times of worship and praise. To keep your times of worship flowing smoothly, obtain a dual-cassette player that will enable you to have your second song cued and ready to go immediately following the first one. Another option is to prerecord your selected songs in order. Some companies even offer prerecorded song medleys.

Most of the companies that make split-track recordings also provide lyric sheets. When teaching a song off a cassette, let the students hear how the song goes, and have them follow along with the lyric sheets. Then have them try it on their own. (You may want to turn the vocal track up just a bit to help them get the feel of the song.)

Appendix 3 offers a list of companies that provide split-track recordings featuring some of the best praise and worship choruses from the past 15 years, as well as the hottest new youth songs.

SINGING WITH INSTRUMENTS
Psalm 150 is the final doxology of praise from the book of Psalms. Within its verses the psalmist explains not only why God deserves our praise but how we can praise God as well. As you study Psalm 150 below, note the variety of instruments mentioned. (I have added italics for emphasis.)

> PRAISE the Lord!
> Praise God in His sanctuary;
> Praise Him in His mighty expanse.
> Praise Him for His mighty deeds;
> Praise Him according to His excellent greatness.
>
> Praise Him with *trumpet* sound;
> Praise Him with *harp* and *lyre*.
> Praise Him with *timbrel* and *dancing*;
> Praise Him with *stringed instruments* and *pipe*.
> Praise Him with *loud cymbals*;
> Praise Him with resounding *cymbals*.
>
> Let everything that has breath praise the Lord.
> Praise the Lord!

Horns, strings, percussion, woodwinds—it's all there. I bet the

Israelites would have praised God with electric guitars and keyboards had they been around in 1,000 B.C.! Dennis C. Benson, author of *Creative Worship in Youth Ministry* adds, "There is no form of music or musical instrument which does not have a place in the worship of God."[1]

We know that young people love music and respond to it as no other age group does. It simply makes sense to utilize the variety of contemporary musical instruments available to complement times of singing, worship, and praise in youth ministry today.

But before you jump right in, remember that learning and coordinating instruments means effort expended in time, expense, and people. Yet I believe the benefits of including musical instruments in the praise and worship of God with youth are well worth the effort.

Evaluating Your Situation

Just as a youth worker plans a service retreat for his or her students with the vision of one day attempting a short-term foreign missions trip, so too should you give your music ministries the same attention to detail, planning, and vision. Before selecting instruments, musicians, and sound equipment, evaluate your ministry situation. Your group size and available resources will influence what you can accomplish. Ask yourself: How many students are in your group? How big is your youth room? Do the acoustics of your room necessitate sound reinforcement, or could you effectively lead music without it? Would a full band be too much for the size of your group at this time? (Perhaps a band is something you could work toward in the future to complement your growth.) Do you have the money to purchase a sound system? Could the money be earned or allocated sometime in the future? Are there students or volunteers in your church ready and willing to lead your group in singing and worship, or will they have to be sought out and trained? How will you train them? What will you emphasize?

I wish I would have asked myself these questions before I plunged into a worship ministry a few years ago. I spent thousands of dollars on sound equipment to establish a band that my group wasn't really even ready for! I found myself trying to justify expenses as my praise band led singing for 20 students who couldn't even hear themselves sing over the instruments! We could have just as easily waited for our group to grow and worshipped with an acoustic guitar, instead of going all out from the beginning.

Therefore, be realistic in evaluating your group and your resources before moving on to the next step. As the Lord leads, plan for the future, set goals, and establish a vision. But don't let unfounded expectations lead your ministry. With the Lord's blessing, your vision will be realized one day!

Selecting Musicians

I discussed the qualifications for the *primary* worship leader in chapter 4. I am more flexible, however, in what I expect from supporting musicians in a youth worship team both in terms of their spiritual maturity and musical ability. Let me explain. I believe the primary song/worship leader is responsible for prompting the students to sing and enter into worship, as well as to lead, train, and disciple those who are playing and participating with him on the worship team. But students and others who wish to be involved in a worship team/praise band experience need room for growth and development. Remember this biblical principle: God takes people where they are; He doesn't wait for them to "arrive." Allowing individuals to grow is what Christian maturity is all about, isn't it?

For a time I had a very talented adult volunteer keyboardist and a student drummer playing regularly on my worship team. The keyboardist struggled in the area of his own personal spirituality (prayer and time spent in God's Word) and shared with me regularly about these difficulties. He was honest and sincere, and I appreciated that.

The young man who was playing drums was a high school student dealing with many of the typical struggles for someone his age. He was also still developing musically. Still, I continued with both of these individuals and tried to support and encourage their growth and ministries. All the while our worship with the teenagers was just fine.

One of the most rewarding aspects of leading worship is having a student begin to lead with you (immature or unskilled as he or she may be), and then watch the Lord grow and develop that person into a worship leader.

Perhaps you don't even have anyone to lead worship with your students, like my friend Jim, whom we discussed at the outset of this chapter. In this case, you must recruit the right people, and this can be a challenge. Typically, I've found that churches that emphasize contemporary praise and worship in the adult service tend to have an abundance of people with musical abilities that are compatible with youth worship . . . and churches that don't, don't. For example, while serving in a church that featured the traditional organ, orchestra, choir, and hand bells, I found it very difficult to find people who played guitar, bass, drums, and keyboards. I'm sure some of you reading this book can relate to that. Dennis Benson has also noted this difficulty. He writes, "Most churches will accept those who play the piano, organ, or trumpet. However, electric guitars, drums, and other secular instruments are looked upon with suspicion."[2] However, through persistent recruitment, I was able to persuade a few willing individuals who played those "secular" instruments to become part of our worship team!

First, try recruiting from within your own youth group. Some students that play instruments may not approach you for fear that they aren't good enough. They may even be shy about playing in front of their peers. Try passing around a sheet of paper that asks students who play an instrument, any instrument, to note it on the paper. Or you might try simply posting a notice on your youth group bulletin board for interested students to sign up on. These nonthreatening ways allow you to tap into the musical potential of your youth group and give you a starting point for recruiting.

Second, try recruiting from within the larger population of your adult congregation. Putting announcements in the church bulletin, visiting adult classes and fellowships, and talking to the minister of music are all good ways to get the word out that you're looking for musicians to serve in your group.

Finally, try recruiting from a local Christian college. If there is one in your area, you should be able to find interested individuals. I've recruited a good number of people for our youth worship team at a local Christian university near my church. They came as a result of word of mouth, chapel announcements, and personal contact.

Selecting Instruments

The resources available to you and the needs of your particular youth group will ultimately determine the instruments you should select. The following is a basic format for determining the instrumental accompaniment that is right for your group, starting with solid lead instruments. By following these ideas, you will be able to create a full worship team/praise band.

Lead Instruments. An acoustic guitar, piano, or keyboard are the most common and effective individual instruments for leading group singing. Let's face it, you just don't see many lone drummers leading group singing. There's a reason for that . . . it doesn't work! Ideally, the person playing guitar, piano, or keyboard should be able to lead the group vocally, but I've also seen situations where a vocalist and instrumentalist worked effectively together.

Additional Vocalist. Adding another vocalist provides balance. Because many songs have guys' and girls' parts, I suggest that you have one male and one female in the primary vocal roles. The basic song-leading arrangement, then, might include a guy who plays guitar and sings and a girl who sings. In your group, the girl may play the instrument; the particulars don't matter. The point is that there is a male who leads males and a female who leads females in the audience. I know this sounds like a basic principle, but I've seen it neglected time and again. Typically I witness two males leading the singing, with one of them trying to lead the girls by mimicking the high sound of a girl's voice or singing beyond their range. It usually just makes everyone laugh and does nothing to add to the group singing and worship experience.

After you have established your basic setup, you may wish to add other instruments and vocalists. (I'm assuming that your basic setup is a male guitar player/vocalist and female vocalist. If you have a female or male who plays piano, then adapt the following suggestions accordingly for adding accompaniment.) Also, I recommend not adding more than one or two of the following instruments at any given time.

Second Acoustic Guitar. The addition of a second or supportive acoustic guitar is usually a natural step for increasing the fullness and variety of your sound. While both guitars can play the rhythm, it works best if the second acoustic guitar player concentrates on playing lead lines, picking, different voicings (such as playing complementary chords up the neck), or using a capo.

I would also suggest that instead of adding a second six-string, flat guitar (which is probably what the first guitar is), experiment with twelve-string guitars or nylon-string classical guitars. You might even consider a mandolin. The addition of these acoustic instruments will give variety to your sound without the heaviness or competitive sound that can occur when using similar six-string guitars.

Keyboards. Keyboards are very versatile instruments for song and worship leading and can complement a single acoustic guitar (or a pair of them) nicely. Keyboards are versatile in several ways. First, they can supply the bass lines that are usually needed to balance the mid- to high-range sound of the acoustic guitar and will allow you to compensate for a bass player until you get one. Second, a keyboardist can provide melodic "fills" that complement and round out your sound, or he can simply provide a base of chords.

The versatile sounds (bells, strings, and so on) that keyboards can reproduce enhance the tone of each song. A variety of keyboards with different capabilities are available. If you have any questions, visit a local music store or just ask a keyboard player in your church. I'm sure you'll have no trouble getting him to talk about his instrument!

Electronic Drum Machines. Some keyboards have good drum machines built in, but you may have to purchase an individual unit for a quality sound. Drum machines are great additions to your acoustic guitars and keyboards (especially if you don't anticipate using a drummer in your situation). I've used them for years to add energy and excitement to upbeat songs. Simply program the beat of a particular song, set its appropriate tempo, and store it in the memory of the machine. You can store literally dozens of patterns in the machine and play them as needed. Drum machines are also nice because you can control the volume. This makes them adaptable to smaller room situations. Finally, drum machines can also be used quite effectively in tandem with a single guitar or keyboard.

Drum machines range in quality and price and can be easily programmed even by nontechnical amateurs like me!

Bass Guitar. The addition of an electric bass guitar will add depth and a "low end" to your sound, freeing up the keyboardist to concentrate more on the melody of your songs. A bass can also enable you to add a lead guitar. If you don't have a keyboard player, a bass guitar can be added to an acoustic guitar, provided that *both* guitars are being amplified.

Drums. If possible, it is a good idea to add bass and drums at the same time because they are complementary instruments that provide a rhythmic base that the rest of your musicians can follow. A skilled drummer can be a tremendous addition to the sound and quality of your worship team. Young people naturally respond to drums, for they add energy and excitement to your rowdy times of singing and can provide a sensitive beat for softer times of worship and praise.

Be careful, however, when choosing your drummer. All the other instruments in the band depend on the timing of the drummer. If your drummer can't keep a beat, he will throw everyone else off, too.

I have also found that while most drummers do well on fast tempo songs, it takes skill and sensitivity for a drummer to accompany slower praise and worship songs. For more information on worship drumming, you may want to consult Mike Kinard's book, *Drums in Worship.*[3]

Lead (Electric) Guitar. I especially enjoy electric guitars for upbeat and energetic songs. Young people really respond to a lead guitar solo in the middle of these types of songs and can literally go wild with enthusiasm! During praise times, electric guitars can significantly enhance the worship when their leads complement the sensitivity of the message and mood of the song.[4]

Other Instruments. For variety you may wish to add additional instruments, such as brass or woodwinds, to your worship group. Adding a saxophone player can add a fun and jazzy sound, while adding a flute can create an altogether different mood. Take advantage of the individual talent you have in your group. If you have a gifted cellist, and you think that he or she will enhance your worship, go for it!

Harmonicas can also be fun to experiment with. A harmonica solo placed at the right time in the middle of a fast song can bring the house down! You might also get creative and try out what I call "fun" instruments that require no real talent to play. Pass out kazoos, maracas, and tambourines to kids in the crowd and let them play with the band! Of course, such shenanigans may not be appropriate for worship times, but they're great for getting kids involved in your lighter times of singing. Let them contribute to your "joyful noise."

Remember, instrumentation can become a distraction if you give it too much attention. Still, a well-orchestrated praise band will energize and enhance your worship and help your students experience the joy of worshipping the Lord.

THINK ABOUT IT

1. Evaluate your situation, filling in the blanks for the following questions:

    How many students are in your group?

    _____

    Does your room and group size require sound amplification, or could you perform effectively without it?

    _____

    What sound equipment does your group possess?

    _____

    What additional equipment might you need to obtain?

    _____

    How much additional money do you estimate you would need to purchase this equipment?

    _____

    If you don't have the funds to purchase the equipment, in what ways might you earn the money?

    _____

    Name several adults and/or students you could approach about participating in student worship.

    _____

2. If money and people resources were not an issue, what would you desire to see your worship team look like within this next year?

3. Pray about God's will for your youth worship ministry and how He might bring it to pass.

6

COPYRIGHT ISSUES

I think God likes to hear music with His name being called out.
David—9th grade

Worship is humbling myself to the Lord and letting Him bring
His Spirit down upon me—letting the Lord talk to me.
Amir—9th grade

know, I know. Just seeing the title of this chapter has probably caused you to break out into a cold sweat. I sense your tension. The mere hint of anything illegal causes most people to cringe. I bet the word *copyright* has caused more self-examination, false justification, and downright guilt in well-meaning song and worship leaders than almost anything else they face in ministry.

Even though we're (notice I've included myself!) simply trying to encourage and minister to others in song, it's just not enough. Unfortunately, we have to mess with all that legal stuff to get proper permission to use a song we've sung all our lives! To ease our consciences, perhaps we say to ourselves, "The good Lord will understand. . . . He'll overlook it just this once!"

But the Bible says THOU SHALT NOT STEAL. When copyrighted material is exhibited, printed, or duplicated without proper authorization from the copyright holder, it is considered stealing. In other words, making song sheets, overhead transparencies, slides, bulletins, or songbooks from copyrighted material is illegal without permission from the author or publisher.

It has taken me years of ministry and hours of investigation to uncover all the facts regarding this somewhat confusing area. I hope that in the next few pages I can help you to understand and comply with the law surrounding this aspect of your worship ministry.

I think we all know the principle of copyrights in general, but just so we can set the record straight, I'd like to cite the official description of copyright from "Circular 1: Copyright Basics" from the Copyright Office of the United States:

> Copyright is a form of protection by the laws of the United States (title 17, U.S. Code) to the authors of 'original works of authorship' including literary, dramatic, musical, artistic, and certain other intellectual works. This protection is available to both published and unpublished works. Section 106 of the Copyright Act generally gives the owner of copyright the exclusive right to do and to authorize others to do the following:
>
> - To reproduce the copyrighted work in copies or phonorecords;
> - To prepare derivative works based upon the copyrighted work;
> - To distribute copies or phonorecords of the copyrighted work to the public by sale or other transfer of ownership, or by rental, lease, or lending;
> - To perform the copyrighted work publicly, in the case of literary, musical, dramatic, and choreographic works, pantomimes, and motion pictures and other audiovisual works, and
> - To display the copyrighted work publicly, in the case of literary, musical, dramatic, and choreographic works, pantomimes, and pictorial, graphic, or sculptural works, including the individual images of a motion picture or other audiovisual work.
>
> It is illegal for anyone to violate any of the rights provided to the owner of copyright by the Act. These rights, however, are not unlimited in scope. Sections 107 through 118 of the Copyright Act establish limitations on these rights. In some cases, these limitations are specified exemptions from copyright liability. One major limitation

is the doctrine of "fair use," which is now given a statutory basis by section 107 of the Act. In other instances, the limitation takes the form of a "compulsory license" under which certain limited uses of copyrighted works are permitted upon payment of specified royalties and compliance with statutory conditions."[1]

(For further information about the limitations of any of these rights: consult the Copyright Act of 1976. or for a copy of "Circular 1: Copyright Basics" consult appendix 1 at the back of the book.)

A very helpful brochure available from the Church Music Publishers Association provides answers to the most commonly asked questions regarding practical applications of the Copyright Law. The CMPA does not wish to copyright the information contained in its brochure in order to better communicate their concerns. For your benefit, I am reproducing a question-and-answer section from the brochure here, but I recommend obtaining a copy for your own records. Again, please refer to appendix 1 for more information.

GUIDELINES FOR THE USE OF COPYRIGHTED MUSIC MATERIAL

Q: What if I'm faced with a special situation?
A: If you want to include copyrighted lyrics in a song sheet . . . arrange a copyrighted song for four baritones and kazoo . . . or make any special use of copyrighted music which the publisher cannot supply in regular published form, the magic word is . . . ASK. You may or may not receive permission, but when you use someone else's property, you must have the property owner's consent.

Q: What if there's not time to write for permission?
A: That makes no difference. Think of copyrighted music as a piece of property, and you'll be on the right track. Plan ahead. Some publishers will grant emergency permission over the phone.

Q: What about photocopies that are now in our church?
A: Destroy any unauthorized photocopies immediately. Replace them with legal editions. Possession of any illegal copies puts you in the

position of harboring stolen goods.

Q: Can I make copies of copyrighted music first and then ask permission?
A: No. Permission must be secured prior to any duplication.

Q: What if I can't find the owner of a copyrighted song, can I go ahead and use it without permission?
A: No. You must have the permission of the copyright owner. Check the copyright notice on the work, and/or check with the publisher of the collection in which the work appears. Once you know the name of the copyright owner, write the CMPA in order to secure an address or phone number.

Q: Is it permissible to print words only on a one-time basis, such as in a church bulletin?
A: No. Permission must be secured prior to any duplication. Using "just the words" makes no difference.

Q: But what about items that are out of print?
A: Most publishers are agreeable, under special circumstances, to allow reprinting of out-of-print items, but again, permission must be secured from the copyright owner prior to any duplication.

Q: Is it necessary to secure permission to perform copyrighted works in church?
A: No. You may perform copyrighted works from legal editions in the course of services at places of worship or at religious assemblies. It's the making of copies that requires permission.

Q: Can homemade songbooks or song sheets be used in churches, Bible studies, or home prayer groups as long as they are not sold?
A: No. Permission must be secured prior to any duplication, for any use whatsoever.

Q: Can I set original or religious words to a copyrighted song (whether religious or secular)—even for my own local church group?
A: Not without permission from the copyrighted song's owner.

Q: Can I make a transparency or slide of a copyrighted song for use by projector?
A: No. The making of a transparency or a slide is a duplication, and

permission must be secured from the copyright owner.

Q: What are the penalties for making unauthorized copies of copyrighted music?

A: The law provides for the owner of a copyright to recover damages for unauthorized reproduction of copyrighted music. These damages include profits of the infringer and statutory damages ranging from not less than $250 to not more than $50,000 per infringement. In addition, prison terms are provided for willful (i.e., you knew what you were doing was wrong!) and commercial infringement. Remember, churches, schools, and non-profit organizations are not exempt!

Q: What about the photocopiers that don't "get caught"?

A: Frankly, we cannot imagine what kind of school, church, or professional musician would derive satisfaction from doing something illegal. They force the price of legal editions higher. They risk embarrassment from those who understand the law; and they risk fines and jail sentences if taken to court . . .

Plainly stated, the making of unauthorized copies of copyrighted material is strictly illegal. However, all music publishers desire to have their songs used in as many ways as possible; so in some cases, permission to duplicate can be obtained. You must contact the copyright owner prior to any duplication.

Feeling convicted? I know I did when writing this chapter. But don't get mad at me. I didn't write the law—I'm only the messenger! But I must admit, it is our responsibility, whether as youth workers or song/worship leaders, to show integrity in this area. Perhaps it's time for some of us to start cleaning house. Need an extra broom?

LICENSING PROCEDURES (GAINING PERMISSION AND PAYING FEES)

Several years back I decided to compile a songbook containing the words and chords to the songs we sang in our youth group. The need arose as student after student began to request the words and chords to the various songs we sang. After the umpteenth time I thought to myself, *There has to be a better way!*

The fact is, there is no easy way of sharing copyrighted material with others. Any way you approach it, it takes some effort. I began by listing all the songs we sang in our group, which at the time was more than 150, and determined to do my best to get proper permission from the copyright owners to use their songs for making songbooks, transparencies, and slides for our group. My ministry associate and good friend, John Hoppis, and I spent a good part of a summer categorizing songs by publisher and writing letters for permission to use the materials. Our letters included the following information:

- Identification of desired songs to be used including name of author, copyright date, and publisher.

- Identification explaining what form the songs would appear and how many copies would be made. For example: "Four songs to be printed in 100 song books; made into four overhead transparencies; and two slides."

- Identification of intended use. For example, we stated that the songbooks would be made available only to students in our group, would not be distributed outside the church, and would not be sold.

In some cases we were granted permission to copy songs in any format for free. In other cases we were required to pay a fee per song or per item copied (such as songbooks, transparencies, and slides); this fee is referred to as the current statutory royalty rate. This royalty fee compensates the author for use of his composition. The current royalty rate for duplicating copyrighted materials can be found out by calling any one of the major music publishers, the CMPA, or the Copyright Office of the United States of America.

I've provided a selective list of major youth music and praise and worship publishers in appendix 3 for your reference as you seek copyright permissions. It is not an exhaustive list, but one that I feel represents the most popular music publishers and resources used by youth workers today.

No More Hassles . . . Christian Copyright Licensing, Inc.

If the copyright licensing procedures I've just described sound like more than you bargained for, I have some good news for you! Christian Copyright Licensing, Inc. (CCLI) may be able to solve about 80 percent of your problem. CCLI coordinates the licensing and usage permissions for more than 700 Christian music publishers, who control the rights to more than 100,000 praise and worship songs.

For an annual fee (it varies depending on the size of your church), churches may obtain the right to use and duplicate the copyrighted materials of companies represented by CCLI. This organization has reduced the inconvenience of licensing for thousands of churches by doing their "dirty work" and has, in the process, likely increased the number of people who now comply with copyright law. Check with your church's minister of music or administrative staff to see if your church is a member of CCLI. Appendix 1 provides more information.

Other Publishers

While CCLI is an excellent resource for most songs, there is still a good chance that your group may want to use copyrighted material from publishers or individuals who are not represented by CCLI. Typically, many youth-oriented publishers are independently operated and may not be a part of CCLI. In such cases you must go through the procedures of writing for permission and possibly paying the fees as mentioned above. But remember, this will probably only account for about 20 percent of the material your group uses.

Don't look the other way when using praise and worship songs in your youth group. I believe that for our music ministries to be truly honoring to the Lord, they should also be permeated with integrity.

THINK ABOUT IT

1. How do you feel when you hear the word *copyright?*

    A) guilty   B) at ease   C) confused   D) angry

2. Commit to "clean house" and destroy any material you have that has not been properly documented. Then seek permission from publishers to use their material within the guidelines they have provided.

3. Write for the brochures listed in appendix 1 to better educate yourself on the details of copyright and licensing.

7

TOOLS FOR TEACHING THE KIDS
YOU'RE REACHING
(SONGBOOKS, TRANSPARENCIES, AND SLIDES)

Worship means to praise God for all the things He has done for us. It's affected me through so many ways I can't fit it on paper. When I worship God through a song I feel God's warmth beside me.

Christy—11th grade

Singing and prayer give me such a high in my spiritual life! I look forward to it! When I close my eyes I feel like I'm talking face to face with Jesus.

Stacy—11th grade

For centuries the traditional hymnbook has been faithfully used to provide worshippers with favorite songs of praise and worship. However, it *may* not be your first choice for the youth group. Let's face it; your average hymnal just doesn't cover all the material you may need for leading today's youth in exciting singing and worship. What methods can you use to teach song lyrics to your students? What "tools" are at your disposal?

Of course the standard songbooks and song sheets still work well, and the more recent innovations of overhead transparencies and slides are helpful, too. You may have the resources necessary to purchase these tools, but if you are working with a youth worker's typically meager budget, you may need to develop your own song-teaching tools.

This chapter is designed to provide you with a number of options and practical resources for obtaining and developing your own music materials. Even if you are already using a particular method, you may wish to experiment with another that helps you expand your capabilities or enhance your quality. Personally, I've found it beneficial to have several methods at my disposal.

PURCHASING YOUR MATERIALS

Over the past 10 years, the availability of helpful materials and worship aids has increased dramatically. Songbooks, slides, and transparencies can be purchased from almost every music and youth resource company. The quality of these materials is usually excellent; they include all proper copyright identifications and permissions for use. However, obtaining all the transparencies, song slides, or songbooks you need will likely cost you several hundred dollars.

You may want to purchase these materials a few at a time to disperse the expenses, or you might share the cost with your minister of music. Still, there is no inexpensive way to obtain them. Appendix 3 lists publishers that provide song-teaching resources.

QUALITY

In general, quality communicates value. For example, because I value my marriage, I spend a significant amount of time and attention building a quality relationship with my wife, Lynne. Or if I value the appearance of my house, then I make sure the yard is kept up (but please don't ask me how often I mow my lawn!). In the same way, if I value the times I have to teach my students, then I will be sure to spend time studying God's Word in order to deliver quality messages that are meaningful, interesting, and effective.

How do students and volunteers perceive the quality of your music ministry? Typically, the song sheets, songbooks, and transparencies used by most youth groups are in poor shape. In a positive sense, well-worn songbooks and transparencies are like the Velveteen Rabbit—they are valuable because they have been used . . . and used . . . and used! However, I believe there is something to be said for quality, too. If you value the singing and worship ministry in your group, why not let your materials show it?

Throw out ripped, torn, and marked-up song sheets and songbooks and obtain new ones. Replace smudged, dirty, and bent transparencies, or use a permanent marker next time you make them so that they can be wiped clean without smudging. If you have misspelled words in your materials or perhaps have improper or incomplete copyright identifications, fix these errors. Store materials properly so that they will stay in good shape. I have often found that some students enjoy writing out transparencies, pulling and filing the songs each week, and generally taking care of the worship materials.

Taking the time to provide your students with quality worship materials will not only benefit them, but it will communicate (through your extra effort) the importance you place on singing and worship in your ministry.

Quality Comparison

Depending on your taste or the resources available to you, you may choose a particular method for teaching song lyrics to your group over another. Yohann Anderson prefers songbooks. He says:

> I prefer books to overhead transparencies because I can relate to them (rather than a theater-style staring-at-a-screen syndrome), and it is more flexible (more songs to instantaneously choose from to fit the mood of a situation). . . . Folks also have the ability to take the lyrics home with them, as well as to sing in small groups. The overhead would not be appropriate in numerous situations (cars, buses, beach, etc.), and is not legal in many. In many situations I've noticed many people cannot see the screen to even know the words to sing. . . . I tend to go toward the high touch as contrasted to impersonal high tech. People bury their heads in songbooks when notes are present. Try to use books or song sheets with no notes. That is one of the reasons why overheads work; they only have the words.[1]

Yohann has in fact published for many years just the kind of songbook he describes here; it is simply called *Songs*.

Songbooks are particularly useful because students can take them home to learn the songs (and hopefully they will bring them back to the youth room). They also provide a variety of songs to choose from at a moment's notice. One disadvantage I have found, however, is that students tend to bury their heads in songbooks while trying to sing. Song sheets create this same kind of problem and need to be replaced frequently.

Unless your group has purchased professional youth songbook compilations that are sturdy and "copyright legal" (like Yohann's), you might want to consider going to transparencies. Keep in mind that quickly prepared transparencies are often hard to read because they are handwritten and become smudged frequently. You can make a quality transparency by using dry-transfer lettering or a photocopying technique. (I'll cover the procedures for making these later.) I like using overhead transparencies because they cause students to look up; they also don't cause as much distraction because students don't have to ruffle through songbooks to locate the next song.

A final teaching tool you may consider is slides. In my opinion, slides are the highest quality method of presenting your lyrics for times of singing and worship and are the easiest to use. By using slides, you eliminate the distraction of turning songbook pages or changing overhead transparencies. In addition, the clarity and effectiveness of slides gives your ministry an appearance of quality that transparencies just can't match.

When I lead singing and worship for camps and conferences, youth workers often comment to me on the difference that slides make. In fact, many churches around the country have put down their hymnbooks and now use slides for their congregational worship.

HOW TO PREPARE, MAKE, AND ORGANIZE YOUR OWN MATERIALS

Someone once said that necessity is the mother of invention. If you're like most song leaders you've probably had to do some experimenting out of sheer necessity to develop your own music materials. Creativity and time will allow you to do just about anything. Still, I'd like to spare you some trial and error by sharing some basic information on making or obtaining your own song-leading tools.

Song Boards

Song boards, otherwise known as the Sunday School posterboard "flip-charts," have been around forever. If you're like many people, they bring back memories of Vacation Bible School. If you simply do not have any available resources (such as overhead or slide projectors, typewriters, computers, printers, or even a copy machine), then song boards may be your most readily accessible option. All you need are several sheets of poster board and some thick felt-tip markers.

Although I do not use song boards in my weekly ministry with students, I do use them when leading singing in places where there is no electric power (like on missions trips to Mexico and other places), or in situations when it's simply not convenient to load up songbooks, overhead projectors, or slide projectors.

Song Sheets and Songbooks

Song sheets and songbooks are another method of teaching and preserving music for your group. Again, proper permission to photocopy copyrighted material *must* be obtained from the owner or publisher and fees must be paid before transferring lyrics to your own materials. (Refer to chapter 6 for copyright licensing suggestions.) When transferring copyrighted songs, remember to note the proper copyright identification, including:

- The copyright symbol ©
- The year of first publication
- The author's name
- The publisher's name
- Statement of permission granted
- CCLI license number (if applicable)

For example:
FACE TO FACE
by Jim Marian

Father, you have prepared a mansion for me
In your eternal home.
It's the place that I've waited for,

The rest that I seek
Where I'll see you face to face.

And it will be heaven there
Yes it will be heaven there
And it will be heaven there
Where I'll see you face to face!

Words and music by Jim Marian
Copyright © 1988 Praise Songs Music
All rights reserved. Used with permission.

Song sheets are convenient for special onetime gatherings, outdoor events, and times where you are leading for other groups, such as at camps and retreats. The benefit of song sheets is that you can put a number of songs on a single page (front and back) at little cost or effort. All you really need to make song sheets is a typewriter or word processor and a copier.

I've already discussed the process of obtaining permission to use copyrighted material for use in "homemade" songbooks in chapter 6. Realize too that homemade songbooks cannot be sold and can only be used in your immediate group or church.

What goes into a good songbook? What are good ways to put them together? Start by compiling material your group likes to sing, then add some material you'd like to introduce students to in the future. In one songbook I made, about 70 percent of the songs were familiar, and 30 percent were unfamiliar to my group.

One impatient student exclaimed, "Hey, Jim, why did you put all these songs in here that we don't know?" I answered the young man with a challenge: "Because whether you believe it now or not, you're going to know every single one of those songs by year's end . . . and like them!" Whether he liked them all, I'm not sure, but I do know he learned those new songs as we introduced them in our worship ministry.

Once you've selected your material, I suggest placing the songs alphabetically by title in your book and numbering either the songs or the pages. I've also found that including indexes that list the songs in alphabetical and topical order can be very helpful to students. Topics such as "up songs," "call-to-worship songs," "Scripture songs," "thanksgiving and praise," "hymns," and "celebration" are all possibilities.

I also include, a third index that gives the Scripture references on which many of the songs are based. It's incredible how many Bible verses can be memorized by students as they learn them in song!

To encourage students to learn the music with their own instruments, I include basic guitar chords above the lyrics in my books. Such "arrangements" must be as close to the original published versions as possible. If you have changed a tune dramatically, you must seek permission from the copyright owner.

To bind your songbook, use a three-hole-punch binding (for loose-leaf notebooks, brads, or portfolios), staples, or permanent bindings (spiral and velobind) that are available at most copy shops.

Transparencies
Using overhead transparencies as a tool for song and worship leading can be very effective for several reasons. First, they allow the worshipper to face the leader, creating greater eye contact than is possible with song sheets or songbooks. Second, they give you the option of keeping the lights in your room at full brightness or at a dimmed level, depending on the mood you are seeking. (Slides generally need a darkened room for best results.) Third, transparencies can be made easily and economically. Fourth, the overhead projection image can be enlarged or reduced depending upon the size of your audience and the size of your screen. If a screen is not available, blank walls usually work just as well.

Most churches have overhead projectors. If you need to purchase one, call a local school district to inquire if it has any used machines; purchasing a new overhead projector can cost up to $400. As for the transparencies, most office supply and stationary stores carry clear plastic transparencies (laser printer and copier compatible) and cardboard frames at reasonable prices.

After obtaining your basic materials, create the layout and lettering. The most professional method for producing transparencies is to print the image right onto the plastic using a word processor and laser printer. If you do not have a laser printer, the next best method is to enlarge the copy from your word processor and photocopy the words onto the transparency. In either case, use a bold, sans-serif typeface in at least 14 to 24 point type. I don't recommend enlarging typewritten copy because the characters are too thin and can't be read easily when enlarged.

If you must handwrite transparencies, use a permanent felt-tip pen (like a Sharpie). When you are writing them, use notebook or graph paper underneath the transparency as a guide. Dry-transfer (rub-on) letters, available at most art stores, or "Kroy"-type lettering can also be mounted on graph paper and then photocopied onto transparencies.

Keep in mind that someone sitting in the back row of your room should be able to read your transparencies easily; if you plan to use them in larger settings, keep this consideration of visibility in mind. Make your transparencies neat and uncluttered. Use two sheets if a song is too long to fit on a single sheet.

Finally, to keep your transparencies in good shape, store them in an appropriate and organized manner. I keep my transparencies in manila file folders arranged alphabetically in a plastic file box. It's a light-weight, portable, and inexpensive way to store your entire music transparency collection. To keep your transparencies from getting scratched or scuffed up from rubbing against each other in the file folders, put a piece of paper between each transparency. You may also wish to mount your transparencies with cardboard frames to protect them from bending.[2]

Slides

My preferred medium for teaching song lyrics is 35mm slides. In my opinion, the finished product of a quality slide can't be beat. Slides can be made or purchased. Here are several ways to create music slides:

Take them to a photo-developing store. Use a computer (a laser printer provides the best results), typesetter, transfer letters, or Kroy letters to create on plain white paper a bold, easy-to-read original of the song you need. Double-check the dimensions of a 35mm slide against your original to make sure that the proportions of the copy will be correct when reduced. Next, take your originals to a local photo-developing store and tell them you would like slides made of your originals. They will use a lithofilm-processing procedure that creates slides with white words on a black background. The cost can range anywhere from $1.50 to $3 per slide. In my experience, this is the fastest and easiest method for making music slides.

Make the slides yourself. Another way to create music slides is to do it yourself. Perhaps you or a student in your group who is involved in photography at school will have the expertise and access to the necessary equipment for developing your own slides. If so, use the following procedure to make effective, quality slides.

1. Create an "original" of your song on white paper with bold, black letters, using the procedure described earlier.

2. Place a 35mm camera with zoom lens on a tripod and center over your original.

3. Light your surface area evenly with four 100-watt bulbs. This will eliminate the possibility of shadows.

4. Use litho film with the ASA set at 12. First, do a short test strip, and remember to shoot your original with as full a frame as possible. Next, shoot at one second, changing the aperture of the camera for each frame that you shoot. (I recommend using a roll with 10 to 15 frames for the test strip)

5. Development: Take a litho developer and mix the A and B parts together. Develop the film for three minutes at 70 degrees.

6. Immerse the film in the stop-bath for 30 seconds, place it in the fix-bath for 4 minutes, then immerse the film in the photo-flow for 30 seconds. Then wipe the film with "photo wipes" *only*. Finally, cut the film and put the shots into slide frames.

7. Determine from your test strip which exposure was the most effective, and use that setting for your other slides.

Finally, you can make "offset" slides that do not require a camera, film, or developing. A large sheet of white paper, markers, or some form of type, and access to a printing shop with an offset printer is all that is required to make up to 24 slides for around $4. For complete instructions on how to make offset slides, consult *The Basic Encyclopedia of Youth Ministry*.[3]

As mentioned earlier, if you don't have the time or desire to make your own music slides (or for that matter, transparencies), you can obtain them from most major Christian music companies and publishers. Some companies also specialize in offering a variety of slides from various publishers in packaged sets. For a listing of these companies, refer to appendixes 2 and 3.

Storage
There are several ways to store your slides. I use aluminum storage boxes that are very sturdy and can hold 100 slides each, arranged alphabetically. I've found this to be an efficient way to store and protect my music slides. Clear plastic slide sheets also work well. These slide or "print" sheets are 8 1/2" x 11", are designed to fit into a three-ring loose-leaf binder, and can hold 20 to 25 slides. These sheets can be purchased at any camera store.

SINGING AND WORSHIPPING WITHOUT THE USE OF WRITTEN AIDS
Although we have discussed many technical details in this chapter, it's worthwhile to remember our ultimate goal: to prompt and encourage students to participate in the joyful experience of worshipping their Lord! Therefore, songbooks, transparencies, and slides are really only aids in helping us attain a greater goal. I've found that the best times of singing—and the most celebrative and intimate times of praise and worship—happen when students are focused.

Song lyrics need to be learned, but written aids can, at times, become distractions that prompt students to stare blankly into songbooks or onto a screen. At times, it seems the lyrics go directly from their eyes to their mouths, bypassing their brains and spirits altogether. By encouraging your students to memorize and sing songs without visual aids, you are helping them to internalize the meanings of those songs and thereby making their expression to the Lord more personal.

Oral methods of learning song lyrics can be just as valuable as visual methods, though more time consuming. Barry Liesch comments:

> In the written tradition people learn by reading. But in the oral tradition people learn through repetition—through repeated hearings—without a printed medium. They listen and memorize. The new material is "caught." In contrast to churches that rely on written material, churches that use oral methods emphasize memorization.[4]

Is it possible for your students to learn to memorize songs? Of course it is! Just think how many of your students can repeat lyrics to songs by their favorite recording artists.

Don't panic. I'm not going to suggest that you throw your transparencies and slides away—at least not yet! Here's a suggestion: When singing songs that are very familiar to your group, avoid using any written or visual aids. For more unfamiliar or new songs, use your songbooks, transparencies, or slides.

When you're leading worship, you may want to group all the songs that may need visual aids at the beginning, then close your worship time with four or five songs that need no assistance. You'll find your students will be more focused on the Lord and less distracted by the tools we sometimes feel are so essential!

THINK ABOUT IT

1.   What tools for teaching songs are you currently using in your ministry? If you were to add another tool, what would it be?

2.   Think of several students in your group who might be interested in making or taking care of materials such as transparencies or slides. What could you do to provide the needed resources and assistance necessary to help them get started in their work?

3.   What benefits would your students realize by memorizing songs? How would it change your singing and worship?

8

WHEN YOUR STUDENTS WANT MORE THAN "KUM BA YAH!"

Worship means taking time out of your busy day to talk to God and let Him know what's going on in your life.

Erica—10th grade

Worship brings me closer to God. It gives me the opportunity to pray in song with words that I might not have been able to think up, but truly mean.

Katie—11th grade

Y ou're a very good song and worship leader for young people. In fact, you're a very good song and worship leader period! At least that's what people tell you—and who are you to argue with the critics? You're always introducing the latest songs on the Top 40 teenage praise-and-worship lists, and you even write your own material once in a while. Your approach is fresh and "Spirit-filled." The songs you choose always seem to have just the right balance and flow. Familiar songs, new songs, crazy songs, and worship songs all naturally blend together to prompt immediate participation from your students. You spend hours each week locating and learning new material you think the young people will really enjoy; this is your ministry, after all. Hallelujah!

If you fit this description, I'd like to congratulate you! It sounds like you're really on top of things. You have my permission to skip this chapter entirely and go on to the next! However, if you are like me and need to work constantly to keep singing and worship up-to-date, meaningful, and alive, then keep reading.

I want this chapter to give you ideas and encourage you as you select and prepare your songs. If your song and worship times have been a little dry lately, maybe you're just in a rut. Webster defines a rut as "a track worn by wheels or by habitual use of something . . . a usual or fixed routine." I know I get in song-leading ruts occasionally when I habitually use the same ol' material I've sung for years without taking the extra effort to improve the quality and content of youth worship. If you're wondering whether you're in a song rut, then consider the following list:

You know you're in a song-rut when . . .

1. All the songs you use are in the public domain.
2. You notice that a song lyric is burned into your screen and remains there after you've turned the overhead projector off.
3. You're the only one singing.
4. The fret board on your guitar is worn thin where you constantly pound out the chords to "Pass It On" and "For Those Tears I Died."
5. Even you begin to yawn during a song.
6. Students start filing copyright violations against you.
7. The parents of your students cheerfully converse with you about the "good ol' days" when they used to sing the songs you sing with their kids.
8. Students begin sabotaging your instruments and hiding the bulbs to your overhead projector.
9. You recall that the last time you taught your students a new song was sometime during the Reagan administration.
10. Even your church's minister of music is more contemporary than you are.

The good news is YOU CAN CRAWL OUT OF YOUR RUT! By learning new material, systematizing your song selection, varying your musical program, and even writing new songs you can escape your doldrums and breathe new life into your worship ministry.

FINDING GOOD MATERIAL

A variety of resources exist to help you expand and improve your collection of song material. Many of these resources are right at your fingertips, while others may require a little more effort to discover. These ideas may not be new to most of you, but I challenge and encourage you to go beyond *knowing* them to *doing* them! I've followed each suggestion personally and have found them to be profitable for collecting good song material.

The College Campus

Students at Christian colleges, seminaries, and state universities can be an excellent resource for uncovering new songs. College students invariably know what's new and hot. If you are a student, seek out others who play an instrument or who might be involved in song and worship leading and exchange material with them. If you're lucky enough to be living in a dormitory on a Christian campus, you owe it to yourself to take full advantage of this valuable time to fellowship with other Christian musicians and worship leaders.

I believe I learned more new songs during my undergraduate days at Pacific Christian College than at any other time since. At least once a week a group of four or five of us would gather together for the sole purpose of sharing songs. We each went to different churches, so there was always an abundance of fresh material to exchange.

Youth Camps, Retreats, and Conventions

Every year my students participate in a number of camps, retreats, and conventions that feature excellent times of singing and worship. Invariably, each event will generate a few great new songs that my students will want me to learn.

I have acquired the habit of bringing a notebook to these events for writing down songs that I'd like to learn (or ones that my students ask me to learn). Sometime during the conference I will try to corner the worship leader and ask him or her for the chords—or at least the key the song was played in. Most worship leaders are very obliging and helpful; they too know how tough it can be to get good songs!

Visit Other Churches

Visiting other churches or youth groups is a great way to learn new songs. If you are a professional youth worker, it may be difficult to get away to another church's worship service, but perhaps two or three visits per year would be enough to gather new material that your group can use.

You may also want to consider visiting different denominations or churches with worship traditions different from your own. For example, if you're from a charismatic tradition, you might want to visit a church or youth group with a noncharismatic tradition, and vice versa. I belong to a noncharismatic tradition, but I enjoy visiting charismatic churches occasionally to take in their worship services. Each time I learn several new songs that work well with my own group.

Youth Worker Song Swap

If you aren't living in a college dorm, or if you just can't seem to get away to visit other churches or youth groups, why not get together with the youth worship leaders from your area for a song swap? Plan a lunch with the purpose of sharing songs with one another. This can provide great opportunities for learning new material and will help you develop a network of friendships with brothers and sisters who share your burden for youth ministry.

Published Song, Praise, and Worship Collections

Perhaps the most obvious way to obtain song material is to purchase it from your local Christian bookstore or order it directly from the publisher. You'll find that each publisher provides a variety of songbooks, song sheets, tapes, and other resources. (If you're interested in ordering a catalog or youth songbook from any of the major Christian praise-and-worship publishers, consult appendix 3.) The resources that have been most cost-efficient for me are the various song-collection books offered by the major publishers. For example, Maranatha! Music, Integrity's Hosanna Music, and Vineyard Ministries' Mercy Publishing all carry excellent praise-and-worship collections, containing hundreds of songs. Youth-oriented songbooks and collections are valuable as well because they often contain material not found in adult praise collections.

SONG CATEGORIES
Just as there are different categories of games for youth activities (such as field games, pool games, team games, elimination games, and crowdbreakers), there are also categories of songs to consider when planning for singing and worship.

When I refer to "categories" of songs, I am not talking about their themes, such as relationships, service, Christian love, prayer, encouragement, and so on. (We'll discuss themes in a later chapter.) Rather, song categories refer to the function served by certain songs during a set. In some respect, song categories are tools that can help you set the tone, focus, and message of a worship time.

Songs fall into six broad categories. You may have your own names for them, but I classify them as follows:

1. *Upbeat songs*—fun or crazy songs that usually have a limited spiritual significance
2. *Celebration songs*—uptempo songs that celebrate the Christian life, attributes of God, and so on
3. *Call-to-worship songs*—songs that encourage the worshipper to focus on God and enter into His presence: usually have a moderate tempo to aid in transition
4. *Praise songs*—songs that extol God, the Christian life, or the attributes of God; generally slower, quieter songs; can speak about, or directly to God
5. *Introspective songs of petition to God*—quiet, intense songs that ask God to help us with our Christian walk or areas of our life
6. *Intimate songs of worship*—intense songs that usually have a slow or moderate tempo; they speak not about us or about life but are exclusively directed to God

These general song categories not only describe the different types of songs but can also help us plan the various phases most commonly experienced in youth worship.

Phase One: Upbeat and Crazy!
Teenagers love to clap, get wild, and shout at the top of their lungs during times of singing. When my students enter our youth room on

Tuesday night, they are usually both tired—from school, practice, homework, after-school jobs—and wired. They need to direct their energy, and unless I focus it, they will spend the whole night just venting it by talking to their friends.

I think all youth workers begin Bible study nights with their students in a disorganized hodgepodge of personalities, emotions, and mindsets. They all have had their hearts and minds focused on a million different things all day long. Our challenge is to bring these individuals together as a group, so that they can ultimately focus on the Lord, allowing Him to minister to them. I have found that music, like no other tool, can accomplish these goals.

Start with several appropriate upbeat, fun, even crazy songs. They create an energetic atmosphere, and when combined with clapping or wild hand motions, the response is usually enthusiastic and unifying. While the lyrics may have some Christian or spiritual content, the atmosphere generated is typically not a worshipful one, nor is it necessarily focused on the Lord. Rather, the atmosphere created tends to focus on the unity of the group itself and celebrates the enjoyment of being together for Christian fellowship (what I have previously referred to as "horizontal worship"). Here are several songs you may consider:

- "Blind Man"
- "Got a Reason for Livin' Again"
- "Ha La La La"
- "I'm Gonna Sing, Sing, Sing"
- "Jesus Is the Rock"
- "King Jesus Is All"
- "Pharaoh, Pharaoh"
- "Shut de Do"
- "Lean on Me"
- "River of Life"

I realize that the song lists I have included in this chapter may sound a little dated. My purpose in including these sample lists, however, is mainly to illustrate the six song categories. I have intentionally used older songs in the hope that my readers will be familiar with them.

Phase Two: Celebration Songs

Celebration songs represent the next phase of worship. The transition from phase one to phase two is smooth because the tempo of celebration songs is usually moderate to fast, and many include clapping. However, celebration songs generally focus specifically on the Lord, which gives the worship leader the opportunity to change the group's focus from one another to God. During these songs, the leader harnesses the enthusiasm generated by the "up" songs and redirects it, minus the silliness and hand motions. Celebration songs encourage students to express the joy of their relationships with God.

Although in this section I discuss using celebration songs as a transition from "up" songs to more solemn praise songs, I also find that concluding a time of quiet, intense praise and worship or wrapping up a powerful message with a time of celebration songs is often a very exciting and appropriate expression as well.

Sometimes as believers we are almost overwhelmed in our spirit by the amazing attributes of our God. Loud and spirited celebration in music can be among the most beautiful and moving times of worship you will share with your students. Here are several songs appropriate for this category:

- "Great Is the Lord"
- "Hosanna"
- "How Majestic Is Your Name"
- "I Will Celebrate"
- "Lord I Lift Your Name on High"
- "I Will Call upon the Lord"
- "I Will Enter His Gates"
- "Awesome God"
- "Jesus, Mighty God"
- "He Is Exalted"

Phase Three: Call-to-Worship Songs

The call-to-worship song is an invocation of sorts. The lyrics to such songs often admonish us to acknowledge the presence of the Lord and begin a time of praise and worship. While I believe true worship can, and does, occur during the celebration phase (and possibly in the upbeat phase), a call-to-worship song helps me lead student worshippers into softer and quieter phases of praise. Call-to-worship songs are usually slower in tempo than celebration songs and flow nicely into the praise and adoration phase. Such songs might include:

- "(Don't You Know) It's Time to Praise the Lord"
- "As We Gather"
- "Come Let Us Worship and Bow Down"
- "First Song I Sing"
- "Psalm 5 (Give Ear to My Words)"
- "Let's Forget about Ourselves"
- "Come and Worship"

Phase Four: Praise Songs

Praise songs are usually moderate to slow in tempo and have a limited musical range (not too high or low). This phase is characterized by open expression as lyrics proclaiming God's praises are sung with adoration, thanksgiving, and joy. Glorifying God in acknowledgment of His person and attributes would be appropriate in this phase, as well as songs describing or extolling the Christian walk. Songs of praise and adoration may include:

- "All through the Day"
- "Father, I Adore You"
- "I Love You, Lord"
- "Jesus, Name above All Names"
- "In Moments like These"
- "Spirit Song"
- "Sweet Adoration"
- "I Want to Praise You, Lord"
- "The Steadfast Love of the Lord"
- "Give Thanks"
- "Majesty"

Phase Five: Introspective Songs of Petition

Just as in prayer, after we have adored our Lord, we often seek His divine intervention in our lives for continued growth and maturity.

Many wonderful worship songs provide a perfect vehicle for these petitions as we ask God to examine our hearts and reveal our areas of sin and weakness. Often these songs are directly from Scripture (Psalms especially); they express man's dependence and need for God's help. I have found that these songs can be a powerful tool for helping students open up their hearts, hurts, and sin before God, even sometimes through humility or tears. These songs may include:

- "Create in Me a Clean Heart"
- "More Love, More Power"
- "Search My Heart"
- "Make Me a Servant"
- "Change My Heart O God"
- "Make Me like You Lord"

I don't include this category of songs in every set, but I do use them frequently, depending on the message or the focus of the meeting.

Phase Six: Intimate Songs of Worship
The final and most intensive phases includes intimate songs of worship. These songs typically are sung in the first person and are directed to God. They express a close, personal relationship between the believer and the Lord. These songs are generally slower in tempo. You may even want to turn down the lights and have students alter their worship posture (close eyes, stand, kneel, lift hands, and so on) in order to emphasize the reverent nature of these songs.

While phase six is a very important phase of worship, remember that not all of your students (particularly new Christians, non-Christians, or younger students) may really understand these songs. The idea of saying to God, "I love You . . . You're beautiful . . . You're worthy to be praised . . . You are exalted" may seem foreign and uncomfortable to some kids. That's OK. In some ways, this level of worship will be an example to them of what their relationship with God could be like. Although you may want everyone to be reverent and focused during these times, don't be frustrated if everyone isn't participating with the same depth. Some students just may not be "there" yet. Songs in this category might include:

- "More Love, More Power
- "Tender Mercy"
- "Cares Chorus"
- "O Lord, You're Beautiful"
- "More Precious Than Silver"
- "As the Deer"
- "It's Your Blood"
- "Stand in Awe"
- "Shield about Me"
- "Humble Thyself in the Sight of the Lord"
- "You Are My Hiding Place"

I have listed here what I consider to be the six phases typically represented in a song/worship time with students in order to give you a format for understanding the flow of an effective worship time and to help in selecting your own material.

Please understand that these phases are in no way the only way to organize a time of worship for youth. You may want to try this structure for a few meetings and then experiment a little to see what flows best with your students. A sensitive worship leader will always tailor his or her song services to the particular goals and needs of the group. Use this structure as a guideline, but feel free to delete or rearrange phases or adapt them appropriately. For example, in one youth ministry where I led worship, I found that my students were unresponsive to upbeat and crazy songs on Sunday mornings. They were usually dressed more formally, and their response was typically groggy at 9 A.M. each Sunday. So I began opening with celebration songs on Sunday; many times I would even skip celebration and start with a call-to-worship song and then go immediately into praise and worship.

We saved our "upbeat and crazy" songs for midweek, a time when they loved it!

SONG SELECTION
Now that we've discussed the different phases of singing and worship, it's time to put it all together to form song lists. Song selection is a very important part of worship leading; it's analogous to using the

right ingredients in a recipe. If you use the right blend of ingredients, the end result will be a tasty product. In the same way, understanding which songs to blend together and in what order to blend them can lead to a moving time of worship.

Strive for a basic repertoire of at least 50 songs (I've listed 56 in the previous examples), and make it a goal to teach two to three new songs per month. This may mean having to drop older songs that your students may be tiring of from your "active rotation." The following lists are examples of song sets you might compile from the songs I've mentioned so far. Each list contains from six to nine songs. In some cases certain song phases may be left out entirely, while in other cases, some song phases are emphasized more. This could be the case for junior high singing-and-worship, where you may wish to have more upbeat and crazy songs and less intimate worship songs.

Possible Song Lists for Junior Highers:

List 1
"Ha La La La"
"Pharaoh, Pharaoh"
"Shut de Do"
"Great Is the Lord"
"First Song I Sing"
"Jesus, Name above All Names"
"Sweet Adoration"

List 2
"King Jesus"
"Got a Reason for Livin' Again"
"Jesus Is the Rock"
"(Don't You Know) It's Time to Praise the Lord?"
"Shine, Jesus, Shine"
"More Precious than Silver"

List 3
"I'm Gonna Sing, Sing, Sing"
"River of Life"
"Lean on Me"
"I Will Call upon the Lord"
"I Will Enter His Gates"
"In Moments like These"
"I Love You, Lord"

List 4
"Blind Man"
"Shut de Do"
"King Jesus"
"Great Is the Lord"
"As We Gather"
"Sweet Adoration"
"Father, I Adore You"
"Cares Chorus"

Possible Song Lists for High Schoolers:

List 1
"Got a Reason for Livin' Again"
"King Jesus"
"Jesus, Mighty God"
"Lord I Lift Your Name on High"
"Come Let Us Worship and Bow Down"
"Shine, Jesus, Shine"
"Jesus, Name above All Names"
"As the Deer"

List 2
"Shut de Do"
"Lean on Me"
"Hosanna""
"I Will Celebrate"
"Don't You Know"
"Spirit Song"
"Shield about Me"
"Create in Me a Clean" Heart
"O Lord, You're Beautiful"

List 3
"Great Is the Lord"
"How Majestic Is Your Name"
"Let's Forget about Ourselves"
"All through the Day"
"Create in Me a Clean Heart"
"Change My Heart, O God"
"More Love, More Power"
"Tender Mercy"

List 4
"Psalm 5 (Give Ear to My Words)"
"Spirit Song"
"In Moments like These"
"I Love You, Lord"
"More Precious than Silver"
"As the Deer"

Again, these lists represent only a fraction of your song-selecting possibilities. When choosing songs, keep your audience *and* the setting in mind. For example, the first night of camp usually requires an upbeat atmosphere because of the high energy level and eager expectations of the campers. In contrast, closing camp communion times would require perhaps nothing but praise and worship. On certain occasions you may wish to take requests from your students. I've found my students enjoy asking for their favorite songs and look forward to the times when I give them this opportunity.

Using the list below, take the time to identify your basic repertoire of songs, and next to each, identify what type of song you believe it to be.

SONG TITLE/SONG CATEGORY (PHASE)　　SONG TITLE/SONG CATEGORY (PHASE)

1. _____ 26. _____
2. _____ 27. _____
3. _____ 28. _____
4. _____ 29. _____
5. _____ 30. _____
6. _____ 31. _____
7. _____ 32. _____
8. _____ 33. _____
9. _____ 34. _____
10. _____ 35. _____
11. _____ 36. _____
12. _____ 37. _____
13. _____ 38. _____
14. _____ 39. _____
15. _____ 40. _____
16. _____ 41. _____
17. _____ 42. _____
18. _____ 43. _____
19. _____ 44. _____
20. _____ 45. _____
21. _____ 46. _____
22. _____ 47. _____
23. _____ 48. _____
24. _____ 49. _____
25. _____ 50. _____

KEEPING TRACK

Do you keep track of the songs you use week in and week out? It's a good habit to acquire for several reasons. First, keeping track of how frequently you use a song will ensure a healthy rotation of material and will prevent you from falling in the song ruts we discussed earlier in this chapter. When I don't follow this method carefully, I tend to select certain songs simply because I know them better than others.

Second, keeping track of songs can reinforce the new songs you introduce by making sure they are repeated frequently enough for your students to learn them. I suggest repeating a new song during three successive sessions following its introduction. This method allows students to learn the song well; hopefully, they'll come to enjoy singing it.

Third, if your church subscribes to CCLI (refer to Chapter 6), you are required to keep a journal that lists each time you make a copy of a song. Check your church's CCLI kit for details.

To keep track of the songs you use while leading worship, copy your lists on Post-It notes. They can be conveniently placed on any instrument for ready reference and are much more convenient than taping a piece of paper on the body of your guitar!

Each week, tally each song on a 3" x 5" card, recording the date it was sung. Keep the cards in a small file box. When you sing the song the next time, simply add the date to the existing card. You can also keep track of your songs on a computer data base or even a loose-leaf notebook.

You may want to divide your song "data base" into three sections: active, less active, and inactive. Songs in the active section may be used about every three to four weeks; this should be your smallest section.

During a typical six-month period, a song should migrate from your active section to your less active section. At that point, it should be sung about once a month (yes, even that current favorite should make way for new material). Finally, after two to three years, a song should become inactive and pulled out of the regular rotation. After that time, it should only be sung for a specific purpose, such as reinforcing the point of the message or to bring back nostalgic memories for your students.

An inactive song will probably be sung only two to four times a year. This may seem needlessly restrictive. After all, most of us are probably singing songs we've known for four or five years on an almost weekly basis. But even worship leaders can experience burnout.

I've found that one of the best ways to keep yourself and your group fresh and stimulated is to maintain a constant rotation of new material.

WRITING SONGS

At first the thought of writing your own songs might be intimidating. You may be asking yourself, *Doesn't that take a lot of talent, creativity, and musical ability?* Answer: No more than preparing a well thought-out, biblically accurate, relevant, challenging, and practical Bible study. Just as you need to have some basic tools to prepare an effective Bible study or message, likewise a little hard work and musical knowledge go a long way in writing effective songs.

Consider the following key principles if you are thinking about writing your own songs for youth singing and worship:

Key #1: What Is Your Reason for Writing?

Most people want to write songs because they feel inspired to do so. Whether from a student's thoughtful reflections or creative insights (perhaps he or she has written a poem that has the potential to be a song) or from your own heart, *inspiration* can come from a variety of places. You must train yourself to look for them. Times of prayer and meditation, personal experience, relationships, Scripture, sermons, or new revelations can all be fountains of inspiration where songs are born. When you get an inspiration, write it down or get it on tape! No matter how cluttered and disorganized the thought, with a little work a phrase of inspiration could be the foundation of a great song.

Songs also arise out of special *needs* or *circumstances*. Someone gets saved and puts his or her feelings down on paper. A group is experiencing tension because of cliques or gossip. Perhaps someone very dear to the youth group has left, causing someone to express the joy of that relationship as well as the pain of the parting. Maybe the Lord has done a special work in your group that requires a song to remember it by. Whatever the need or circumstance, don't hesitate to express it in song. Often such personal songs have great meaning to the groups they are written for and bring an added depth to times of worship.

On some occasions you will simply have a desire to write a song about something without necessarily being inspired about any one thing in particular. This kind of "deliberate" song writing is a valid pursuit in itself; not all people have endless springs of inspirational creativity flowing from their veins. I tend to be a deliberate song writer. I had an idea (call it inspiration if you want, but I think it was just a plain, old idea) to write a song that would encourage students to give their day to God as they experienced Him in a variety of ways. The song talked about obeying Him throughout the day, acknowledging Him in creation, and seeking to know Him by experiencing His wisdom and peace. I entitled this composition "Morning Song," and it became one of my students' favorites.

Key #2: Developing Lyrics
Sometimes a title will shape the lyrics of a song, or perhaps a memorable phrase or chorus. Good song lyrics are descriptive and naturally paint word pictures that can be easily understood, felt, and grasped by those singing the song. Good song lyrics make sense and are focused on a central theme. For example, Tom Coomes's call-to-worship song "As We Gather" encourages individuals to experience God by worshipping Him. It does not talk about service, confession, thanksgiving, or forgiveness. It remains consistent with its central theme, and as a result, students easily understand, feel, and sing it.

Work at rhyming and word choice. A thesaurus and a rhyming dictionary are good sources for locating penetrating words and creative words that rhyme. Avoid clichés and lines that appear often in other worship songs.

Effective, moving lyrics come from the heart. If they do not mean anything to you, why should they mean anything to those you teach? Songs written with honesty and integrity will affect others because we all share common emotions and experiences to some degree.

Songs may contain a repetitive chorus to complement several verses, or they may consist solely of a memorable chorus of a few lines. For example, John Wimber's "Spirit Song" has a chorus and several verses, while Terrye Coelho's song "Father, I Adore You" is a simple chorus consisting of a few repetitive lines. Both songs are memorable and have been enjoyed by thousands within the body of Christ.

"Hooks" are memorable lines, phrases, or choruses that provide continuity and flow to songs. For example, the line "I will trust in You," from the song "You Are My Hiding Place," as well as the phrase "Shine, Jesus, Shine," from Graham Kendrick's song of the same name, are good examples of hooks.

Polish your song lyrics until they are as good as they can get. Remember, effective song writing is 90 percent perspiration and only 10 percent inspiration. You may finish some songs in the course of a day, while others may take weeks or even months to complete.[1]

Key #3: Writing Music

Many times you will come up with a tentative tune to accompany the lyrics you have written. I suggest recording this initial melody and lyrics on a tape player, no matter how unfinished the song may seem. Then try to figure out the chords or melody on your instrument or get with a musician who can help you get the basic music down on paper.

The music should move from chord to chord within a framework compatible to the key in which the song is written. Depending upon your musical ability and style, the arrangement can be as simple or as complex as you like. Suffice it to say that knowing how to achieve musical integrity and balance is essential for writing good songs.

It may also be important to consider how the music complements the message of the lyric. For example, a worship song on the subject of confession and forgiveness might be communicated best with soft and slow music rather than with a fast-paced rhythm and clapping. On the other hand, you may have several different feelings and emotions to communicate that would need to be reflected in the music.[2] For example, Donn Thomas and Charles Williams's praise song from Psalm 3, "Shield about Me" is basically a slow, melodic song, but the music picks up intensity with the hook, "Hallelujah, hallelujah, hallelujah / You're the lifter of my head."

Writing songs for your own group can be a rewarding endeavor. Just think how encouraged a young person would be to have his or her songs actually sung by their peers in the youth group! Also, the feelings of ownership that "in-house" songs bring to a group are sure to encourage added participation!

THINK ABOUT IT

1. How consistently do you introduce new songs to your group? Circle the appropriate response:

    A) Hardly ever (in a bad rut!)
    B) Occasionally (every other month or so)
    C) Consistently introducing new material

2. Who are some fellow worship leaders you could get together with and share material? Where are some places you could go to learn new material? Write them down and make an effort to make some appointments and visits this month!

    _____
    _____
    _____
    _____
    _____

3. Is your music library up-to-date? Is it balanced with both praise-and-worship and good youth group sing-a-long material?

4. What song categories do you keep in mind when organizing your material for worship? What blends of categories do your students respond to best?

5. What is your method for keeping track of the songs you sing with your students week in and week out? If you're not using a method, which one suggested in this chapter would be most helpful to you?

6. Have you written your own songs? How have your students responded to them? Do you encourage your students to write songs for the youth group to sing? What could you do to encourage them to begin?

9

Our Motto: Be Prepared!

As it says in the Psalms, "sing to the Lord"! Worship is my way of asking for forgiveness and praising His name. It's like praying while singing a tune. There is nothing better than awesome worship.

Peter—12th grade

Worship is one of my closet times with God. It makes me feel really good and I feel clean and refreshed after worship.

Kevin—8th grade

Sunday morning caught you by surprise again. But, hey . . . you had a hectic week! You spent hours studying for that lesson on "Common Teenage Misconceptions about the Millennial Reign of Christ" and even more hours searching for the church's earthball for Wednesday night's recreation. On top of that you endured yet another exciting church board meeting that lasted till midnight only to be awakened early the next morning by a procrastinating student who wanted to borrow several of your books for a research paper due that day.

What's more, your car broke down, the cat ate your goldfish, and you forgot your mother's birthday. Just another typical week in the life of a youth worker.

Well, back to Sunday School. Here you are, standing in front of your 30 wide-eyed high school students, stumbling your way through another Sunday morning worship time. You wanted to teach them that new song you learned, but you didn't have time to practice it. You're not sure you have all your visual aids in order, and you didn't have time to tune your guitar. Although they'll probably forgive you, you still feel guilty for not giving it your best.

Sound familiar? It does to me. We all have bad mornings or weeks, but hopefully preparedness, not unpreparedness is the rule of our ministries. Many youth workers have a "wing-it" mentality and excuse their lack of planning because they are just working with "kids." This mindset is not only unbiblical, but it will also compromise the integrity and quality of our ministries. Whatever happened to *preparation?*

Like some of you, I was a Boy Scout. Our motto was BE PREPARED! We spent countless hours earning merit badges in order to prepare ourselves for life's various challenges. Camping skills, first aid, citizenship, personal finances, cooking, life saving, and environmental science were all suppose to train us to be prepared. I even made it to Eagle Scout!

Now, one might imagine that with all this preparation I would always be prepared and organized, ready for virtually any situation. Wrong! Just ask my secretary. She has a sign posted by her desk (for my benefit) which reads: "A lack of planning on *your* part does not constitute an emergency on *my* part."

Are you prepared as a worship leader? Or do you occasionally slip into a rushed, unorganized state? I challenged myself to be consistent in my preparation for song and worship leading in order to give both God and my students the very best that I have to offer. Tom Coomes, president of Maranatha! Music, encourages worship leaders to diligently prepare themselves. He says, "If you will approach your preparation with the same seriousness that a pastor uses in preparing his message, you'll see wonderful results."[1]

Do you approach your worship preparation with a determination to cover as many details as possible? I'm reminded of the words from Proverbs 27:12, which tells us that "a sensible man watches for problems ahead and prepares to meet them. The simpleton never looks, and suffers the consequences" (TLB).

The information in this chapter is designed to aid you in your preparation for effective, hassle-free song leading.

LEARNING YOUR MATERIAL

A mistake many of us make is to learn new material two minutes before trying to teach it to others. When rushed or unprepared, I have pressured not only myself to learn the music, but accompanying musicians as well. I've placed music in front of my keyboardist and have told him to follow me as I set out to teach the song to my students. While talented (and patient) musicians may come through with last-minute heroics, you shouldn't make this a habit, especially if you want to keep your musicians.

The rule I now follow is never to lead a new song that I don't know 100 percent. I've blown it too many times trying to wing a song before a group. Missed chords or messed-up words have only detracted from the worship and embarrassed me! I'm not suggesting that you must be perfect; it's good for students to see that we are human now and then. Still, there are times when mistakes truly do take away from the singing. So, as badly as you may want to teach that new song, it's better to sing an old one than to do a new one poorly.

Memorize, Memorize

I believe all of us can memorize better than we think we can. Ever learned a semester's worth of material the night before the final exam? I thought so! Still, many of us are intimidated by the thought of having to memorize all the words and music to every one of those youth group songs. We rely on songbooks, or put chords above the words on our transparencies, or devise some other ingenious way of leading the songs without having to memorize them.

I suggest memorizing your material for several reasons. First, with your eyes removed from a book or chord chart, you will be able to worship along with your group.

Second, memorizing your material increases communication with your audience. Eye contact and facial expression are a worship leader's tools for engaging a student's attention and participation. When students sense the leader is not in control, it makes them uncomfortable as they follow.

Third, memorization allows you the flexibility to add or delete songs as the Spirit leads. I can't begin to count the number of times I've added a song or two to my prepared "set" because the mood of

119

the worship seemed to dictate it. If I had to fumble with charts or book pages, it would have destroyed the spontaneity.

By memorizing songs as you go, you'll soon be surprised how many you'll actually learn. Over the years my mental song file has grown to somewhere between 150 and 200 songs. Of course, if I haven't done a song in a year or so, I may need to refresh my memory, but it often comes back to me in no time. Finally, memorization will allow you to relax and lead with confidence.

Now that I've laid down the law, let me season it with some grace. While I see tremendous benefits for the primary worship leader to have the songs memorized, it is not as important for accompanying players. Instrumental players function primarily in supporting roles and can depend upon written music or lyrics without distracting the participants from worshipping. However, I still feel that memorization will enhance their own personal worship experience and will thereby contribute to corporate worship as well.

Don't, however, let your failure to memorize material prevent you from leading. It's OK if you still need to follow a book for certain songs. I believe that memorizing your material will benefit you in the long run, but if you need assistance in the short run, then by all means indulge. I know I do on occasion!

Practice Pays Off

Without practice, how can you improve or even maintain your skills? Most of us need to continually practice our material and work on our instrumental technique to improve our quality and effectiveness. It's that simple. Without practice we can become complacent with our musical gifts and risk the possibility of sacrificing excellence for mediocrity. Be the best you can be with the talents God has given you.

Ronald Allen and Gordon Borror, coauthors of the book *Worship: Rediscovering the Missing Jewel,* comment, "We must remember that God is not the author of mediocrity. He demands our best. If, before God, that which some may consider to be junk IS our best, surely He understands and is appropriately responsive to our worship and praise."[2]

Practicing individually or with your worship team is important in order to improve. Internationally recognized worship leader Graham

120

Kendrick comments, "One minimum standard to set . . . is whether a person can maintain the flow of worship without constant interruptions caused by technical ineptitude. On the instrumental side of things there is a minimum standard below which the playing starts to drag the spirit of worship down, rather than lift it. . . . With practice and a determination to be a good workman, a musician of average ability can provide all that is necessary, and find that his or her offering is a positive help rather than a hindrance to worship."3

Kendrick's words encourage me, especially since I am only an average musician. Still, I have learned to be an effective worship leader with students because I have taken the time to practice. Challenge yourself to improve little by little on your instrument. If you play guitar, experiment with different chord positions to give yourself more flexibility and variety. If you play keyboards, experiment with different fills or parts.

There was a time when I couldn't play a blues rhythm on guitar, and it kept me from playing a lot of fun material for my students in a style they really enjoyed. People repeatedly showed me the basic progressions, but I just couldn't get it. I literally had to force myself to learn the blues rhythm over a period of a year. Thanks to persistent practice, I can finally play it.

On the other hand, when I have not been so devout in practice, it has upset my song and worship leading ministry. For a period of about two months I was distracted with other concerns in my ministry and neglected reviewing my music material. During that time there was not a meeting where I did not either forget a lyric or a chord to a song. My mistakes brought the enthusiasm, momentum, and worshipful mood to a screeching halt.

Lesson learned: Personal practice pays off!

If you're part of a worship team, you probably already know the necessity of scheduling regular practices as you learn to work and blend together. If you're starting a worship team and are wondering what to emphasize or what to include in a practice session, here a few suggestions you may find helpful:

First, make sure your worship team members will commit to regular rehearsals. You'll get nowhere with uncommitted people, whether adults or students.

Second, if you're the leader, make sure all the sound equipment, music, and other preliminary details are taken care of before your team arrives. In this way you'll be able to concentrate your time and energy on learning and rehearsing the music, instead of wasting it rounding up music or searching for microphone cables.

Third, emphasize a less-is-more approach to teamwork and blending. For example, if your instrumentalists start jamming solos every time several "free" bars of music (that is, music with no lyrics) show up on the page, you will create nothing more than distracting noise! If your instrumentalists understand their roles as accompanists, you will produce a better sound and ministry. Webster defines accompaniment as "subordinate music to support a principal voice or instrument."

Fourth, provide your musicians the music and tapes of the songs in advance. In this way, each musician can learn his or her own musical parts (the tapes can be very helpful). Your rehearsal then becomes more of a "coming together" to work on style, blend, and song dynamics. This will not only make your rehearsals more enjoyable and rewarding (since there will be no waiting around while one person "pounds" out their part), but you'll cover more material as well.

Fifth, allow everyone on the worship team to give input. Whether suggesting new songs or ideas on specific songs, by allowing everyone to contribute you will build a stronger worship team. Remember, this is *their* ministry, so give them ownership. Of course, the leader must give direction and use discernment when taking suggestions, but allowing for others to give input is what teamwork is all about!

Sixth, whether individually or as a team, I suggest attending a worship leaders training session or seminar at least once a year if possible. Different music companies such as Songs and Creations and Maranatha! Music offer very helpful seminars geared to encourage, train, and challenge song and worship leaders. Even an informal workshop given by a music professor or minister of music can be beneficial because it will focus and stimulate your team.

PREPARING YOUR SOUND EQUIPMENT, INSTRUMENTS, AND VISUAL AIDS

As you prepare to lead a group of students in worship, it is wise to ask yourself, *What could go wrong?* This question does not indicate a lack of faith, pessimism, or an expectation of failure. Rather, it should alert you to consider carefully the many details involving your sound system (if you use one), instruments, and visual aids. These technical components of your music ministry have the potential, if not properly prepared, to cause a great deal of distraction.

Sound Equipment

If you can't operate and troubleshoot sound systems, then I suggest finding someone who can. A good sound person is not only capable behind the board but is conscientious in keeping the sound equipment in good repair. Youth rooms can be dangerous places for expensive sound equipment. Each time a microphone is dropped, a cable is tripped over, or a speaker is hit by some flying object, damage can occur. Without regular maintenance checkups, the potential for something breaking down right before or even during a worship time increases.

I would suggest implementing a bimonthly maintenance check on the working condition of your speakers, cables, adapters, sound board, and microphones. Or better yet, make condition assessments a part of your normal set-up or break-down procedure. I find that at least a couple times per year I have to take equipment in to be serviced or replaced.

Perhaps you can locate someone in your church who is qualified to work on sound equipment and who would be willing to donate his or her services. I wouldn't let just anyone work on my sound system, but I have, on occasion, found competent individuals willing to donate their time and talents.

Second, preparation also includes setting your equipment up in advance of the students' arrival. I know this may sound elementary, but how many times have you found yourself setting up microphone stands and connecting cables minutes before the start of a meeting? Give yourself enough time to have everything prepared in advance so as to avoid being unnecessarily rushed or distracted. After all, your first priority is the students, not the sound system or music. I like to be free when students arrive so I can talk to and hang out with them; I prefer not be tied up (sometimes literally) in cables and plugs.

A final consideration in preparing your sound system is the all-important sound check. Again, be sure to give yourself enough time before the students arrive to get a good sound balance and to make sure everything is working properly. Whether you're working with a tape player, a guitar, or an entire worship band, sound checks are crucial for creating a well-balanced sound; they also help you avoid musical and technical distraction.

Instruments

Over the years I have experienced innumerable instrument problems. Any instrument "failure" during worship is a distraction, but about 90 percent of these problems could have been avoided with some advance preparation. For example:

- strings break in the middle of a worship set because they were not replaced regularly
- pianos are desperately out of tune because of negligence or mishandling
- drum equipment and/or sticks break during a singing time
- the right adapter to plug an instrument into the system cannot be found

Instruments require tender loving care. Replace worn parts before they get to the point of breaking or going bad. Tune your instruments individually and with other instruments before you lead singing and worship. Have extra or backup equipment (cords, adapters, picks, drumsticks, and so on) available whenever possible. Anticipate any difficulties or problems you may encounter before leading. For example, there was a period of time when I would break strings on my guitar almost every week. (Our worship ministry must have been going well because Satan was certainly trying to defeat it!) I got to the point where I had a backup guitar ready for just such emergencies. A quick change of guitars is much less distracting than having to stop the singing for a string change!

Visual Aids

Whether your group uses transparencies, slides, songbooks, or song sheets, it pays to make sure they are organized and properly prepared beforehand. If you are using slides or transparencies, make sure the order is correct and that nothing is turned upside down. Even though it's laughable when inverted lyrics appear on a screen, it only distracts from the focus of singing and worship and communicates disorganization.

When teaching new material, have new transparencies and slides made in advance. I've often procrastinated in doing this task, and as a result my students have been deprived of learning new songs.

When directing the song selection from up front, you may wish to have a vocalist or a student change transparencies for smooth transitions. For slide projectors, you may look into purchasing a foot pedal that allows you to change slides from up front. When using others to operate your visual aids, communicate clearly how to run the projector properly as well as how to focus and troubleshoot, if necessary. Just as in the case of instruments, have backup cords, bulbs, or even spare projectors available for emergencies.

Prepare your visual aids properly with appropriate copyright identification (see chapter 6). In addition, check for spelling errors in your material. Such errors are often noticed by students and distract their attention.

PREPARE THROUGH PRAYER

To be sure, all preparations are important, even critical, for responsible worship leading. However, all of our best efforts are in vain until we seek the Lord in prayer. In an article entitled, "Leading People to an Encounter with God," Chuck Smith, Jr., pastor of Calvary Chapel in Capistrano Beach, California, comments:

> Worship is too important to attempt without prayer and planning. And if we're going to pray, then we're also going to have to trust God to answer our prayers and work within people as we attempt to lead them. We can't conjure up God, but we can take Him at His word. If He promised to be with those who come together in His name, then we can begin our work knowing God's Spirit is already at work in the hearts of worshippers.[4]

Prayer, therefore, brings the spiritual dimension of worship leading into its proper focus. All the practical considerations of preparation and planning are ultimately dependent upon the Lord as He works both in us and through us.

In her book *Up with Worship,* Anne Ortlund similarly encourages worship leaders to dedicate themselves to prayerful preparation. In speaking of the final preparations for a time of worship, which she refers to as the "holy huddle," she remarks:

> Sunday School starts at 9:30, right? . . . Eight-thirty, then, should be about right for the final huddle. . . . You're saying you went through it . . . and now it's got to get into the hearts of everybody who's going to help it happen. It's time for the priests to kindle the fire on the altar! It's time to pray it in, work it up! Besides, maybe God's Spirit has some last-minute change or insertion which will lift, or delightfully surprise, or add meaning.[5]

Do you have your own version of the "holy huddle"? Do you get with your worship team to pray fervently for the Holy Spirit to work in the lives of your students through the worship and your whole meeting? Allowing the Lord to lead your preparation is essential if His power and presence are to be known and experienced during your worship time. If you're neglecting this all-important aspect of spiritual preparation, then my friend, it's time to huddle up!

THINK ABOUT IT

1. Describe your reaction to the following statement by Tom Coomes: "If you will approach your preparation with the same seriousness that a pastor uses in preparing his message, you'll see wonderful results." Is his statement a realistic one for youth song leaders? Why or why not?

2. Do you feel more comfortable memorizing songs before leading them, or do you prefer using songbooks with words and music? What are the drawbacks and benefits of each approach as you see it?

DRAWBACKS	BENEFITS
1. _____	1. _____
2. _____	2. _____
3. _____	3. _____
4. _____	4. _____

3. Describe your feelings when you try to lead singing and worship unprepared.

4. After reading this chapter, what can you begin doing to improve your preparation?

10

THE SETTING: MOOD AND ATMOSPHERE

Worship makes me feel wanted and loved . . . and with this feeling I want to share with many others so that they will see God today and in the end.   *Patrick—11th grade*

I feel closer to God when I'm singing than at any other time. I love lifting up praises to Him. Sometimes I feel like I could just reach out and touch Him.

Faith—9th grade

We know that a student's day is busy and typically pressure-filled. Maybe he doesn't get along with his teacher, or she is failing math. Perhaps he has an unreasonable list of after-school chores, or she puts in four hours at an after-school job. Then add pressure from parents, demands from coaches, struggles with peer relationships or a budding romance, and you have got one stressed-out kid! Yet this is nothing more than a typical day in the life of your average teenager. Often your students bring their excess energy, distractions, anxieties, pressures, and concerns of the day into the youth room for Wednesday night Bible study. They may or may not be disposed to what you have planned for the evening.

Some nights they may be as rowdy as a crowd at a football game, then the next week in the mood for a candlelight dinner! Therefore, being sensitive to provide an appropriate mood and atmosphere to spark student participation is necessary when planning your times of singing and worship. It is my hope that this chapter will not only help you identify various moods that are conducive for singing and worship, but also assist you in creating an environment that says, "Come and participate."

ROOM CONSIDERATIONS

How would you describe the environment in which your students meet and worship? You may meet in a portable classroom, church basement, home, amphitheater, gym, Sunday School classroom, state-of-the-art youth facility, church sanctuary, school classroom, or perhaps something else. You may or may not be in an ideal venue, but it is still important to assess your environment and evaluate the impact it will have on your worship. I encourage you to evaluate your general room environment by considering the following statements:

What Does *Your* Room Environment and Setup Communicate to Students?

WELCOME	or	ENTER AT YOUR OWN RISK!
PLEASE PARTICIPATE	or	JUST OBSERVE
RELAX AND BE YOURSELF	or	BE ON GUARD; WE'RE WATCHING YOU!
COMFORTABLE	or	STERILE
TOGETHERNESS	or	SEPARATION
WARMTH	or	COLDNESS
YOU BELONG	or	YOU'RE TOLERATED
THIS IS YOUR ROOM	or	THIS IS THE CHURCH'S ROOM
EXPRESS YOURSELF	or	BE RESERVED

What does your present meeting room communicate to your young people? Ideally, a room in which the students feel comfortable and

130

have a sense of ownership will facilitate participation and enhance the effectiveness of your music ministry. If the ambiance says "participate," people will.

If your atmosphere of your room communicates a negative message, then the call to praise and worship will be hindered. For example, a chilly, poorly ventilated church basement with inadequate lighting and metal chairs is a cold, sterile environment and may make it difficult for the students to open up and participate. Try brightening this atmosphere with some rugs and pillows or padded chairs, improved lighting, and a few fans. I've known youth groups in these kind of settings that have done just that! In fact, I'm sure you can think of a number of things you could do to improve the environment of your facility. Perhaps one of the easiest and least expensive ways is to consider your seating arrangements.

Seating

Seating is a very practical consideration for achieving full participation in singing. Various options may be used for a variety of desired atmospheres. While some setups are applicable for any given situation, others are more specific and designed to facilitate a certain mood. Here are some ideas to consider:

1. Move Group Members in Close. Studies indicate that closeness stimulates participation. When people are separated or isolated from one another by space, participation is reduced. For example, students who sit in the back row and with a chair between them and the next person may be subtly communicating that they are not interested in participating in singing or interacting with others. Those who sit all bunched up in the front row are more than likely prepared to give it all they've got! Get rid of those empty chairs!

When setting up chairs, space them so that they touch each other. The spacing between rows should be tight yet comfortable. This closeness will facilitate group participation because the proximity will not only allow students to hear one another sing but will provide a sense of community as well. Also, get in the practice of setting up *fewer* chairs than you think you will need. Empty chairs tell kids that their friends had other more important things to do than participate in youth group and that they are "out of it" for being there. Besides, the empty spaces will likely be left in your front row and around your back row nonparticipants, which are the worst possible places! It is much better to add chairs during your meeting, for it communicates to students that youth group is growing and happening!

Second, compare your room size to the size of your group. Can you imagine trying to lead an exciting and meaningful time of singing for 20 kids in a room built for 200? It would be quite a challenge to say the least. If you find yourself in a room substantially larger than the group you're going to lead, either change rooms or make the room feel smaller. Partitions, portable chalkboards, or other barriers can be used to make a room feel smaller and provide that sense of closeness.

Third, to bring together the entire group, whether 20 or 200, remember to play to the back row. If you are able to communicate effectively with the "back row bunch" and get them to participate fully, then you should have no trouble at all grabbing the entire group's attention.[1]

2. Experiment with a Variety of Seating Arrangements. Seating arrangements can vary depending upon the atmosphere you wish to create. Straight rows may suggest a linear, "school room" feel, but this setup can work for moods that are more upbeat. Clapping and hand motions are usually enough to involve a group in singing; this activity will lessen the negative impact that sitting in straight rows may create.

Semicircles and circles are usually the best seating arrangements for encouraging group participation in singing. Being able to see other faces provides groups with a sense of unity and enhances communication because of the increased eye contact. For larger groups, of course, you simply may not be able to get 80 to 150 teenagers in a huge circle or semicircle. For larger groups, an amphitheater-type setup works best, with rows of chairs arranged in a semicircle.

Sitting on a carpeted floor or using pillows is another seating option you may consider. Whether in a home or in a youth room, sitting on the floor naturally relaxes students and helps them to drop their guard. Typically, students do not sit on the floor in school, so when they are encouraged to do so at youth group it communicates a message of "just be yourself, relax, and participate." Both upbeat and quieter times of singing are facilitated by this method of seating. However, watch out

for the "dozers." Sitting on the floor makes it easy for your nonparticipants to simply lay down or lean back so far that they effectively
remove themselves from the group.

Lighting

Lighting must be more than just a way for students to see. Proper use
of lighting can be your greatest tool for creating a mood and atmosphere for dynamic youth singing. Allen and Borror comment:

> Light adds life to an atmosphere when it is properly placed and used.
> Poorly placed or poorly controlled light can be most distracting. Light
> can add dramatic emphasis . . . a sense of expectancy and anticipation.
> Dimming lights for certain times can help create a sense of quiet and
> introspection. An underlit building can actually be depressive. . . . 2

What is the quality and capability of the lighting in your room? Do you
have fluorescent or incandescent lighting? Do you have burned-out
lights that need replacing? Can you dim the lights? I realize that the
majority of youth rooms do not have lighting that can be controlled.
While this is not ideal, there are creative ways to compensate.

If your room has only fluorescent lighting, try placing several well-
positioned lamps around your room. With the fluorescent lights turned
off and one or more lamps turned on, you will create a softer atmosphere that will be quite beneficial for quieter times of praise and worship.

Dimmer switches can also be valuable for changing the mood of a
room and may be an inexpensive addition to your existing lighting.
Finally, candles are a great way of providing light for intimate times of
sharing and worship. A dark youth room lit only by several candles
will produce an atmosphere your students will immediately respond to.
Used sparingly, candles are very effective for special times of worship
and sharing.

Acoustics

Some rooms are acoustically "live" while others are "dead." For example, one youth ministry I led had about the most acoustically lifeless
room possible. Thick wall-to-wall carpet, low acoustic ceilings, and

sound-absorbing wall panels made this room a sound-deadening sponge! In another ministry I had just the opposite experience. This particular place was acoustically alive. The ceilings and walls were high and solid, and we led singing from a wooden stage. The energy level of the students as they sang was at times electric as the sound reverberated throughout the room.

If possible, look for meeting places that are acoustically bright. Look for reflective surfaces (such as hard floors, ceilings, and walls) to enhance sound liveliness. You can always add carpet, rugs, or acoustic wall panels to help control echo, if needed. The point to remember is that acoustically live rooms give back sound to those singing. (Ever wonder why you sound so good singing in the bath-room or the shower?) Hard surfaces reflect sound and naturally encourage volume and participation for singing.

Distractions
Most rooms have elements that distract from the singing and worship experience. One of the things I do when I go into a room (whether it's my own or that of another church or camp) is to identify possible dis-tractions and do what I can to reduce or eliminate them. What distrac-tions might you encounter in your room or with your equipment? Here's a list that might help you get started:

- Light coming through a window that washes out your screen
- Curtains or blinds that don't block out sunlight
- Poor ventilation or noisy air conditioners
- Sofas or other conversation "corners" (teenagers love to "tune out" in them, so beware!)
- Flickering lights
- Buzz in the sound system
- Doors behind the up-front area where people exiting or entering will be seen by all
- Clocks (*you* need to monitor the time, but your students don't)
- Anything the students can read, hold, shred, or fidget with instead of focusing on the worship

In a particular ministry where I served, the high schoolers met in a room called the Valley Room. Our church was located on a hill over-looking an entire valley in the suburban Los Angeles area. The Valley Room boasted an entire wall of curtainless windows, which gave the room a beautiful view of the valley (that is, when you could see it on smogless days). I soon discovered that leading singing in the Valley Room was quite challenging. I found that my students were constant-ly distracted because they were busy daydreaming as they looked out the windows. It was also impossible to darken or change the mood in the room because of this wall of glass.

I attempted to verbally encourage my students by saying futile things like, "Hey guys, let's really try to focus in on the words to this song." But it didn't work. They continued to stare blindly out the win-dows. I then tried rearranging the chairs, but to no avail. The only alternative was to spend the money to put blinds over the windows. Not only did this give us the ability to darken the room, but the blinds took away a cold draft and eliminated a major distraction that hin-dered my students from focusing on the Lord during worship.

What are the distractions in your room? Have you begun to identify them? What could you do about them? These questions are important to consider as you prepare an atmosphere for your room that will be most conducive to full participation in singing and worship, not to mention enhancing the room for your meetings as a whole.

PUTTING IT ALL TOGETHER

So far we've discussed how to create an environment for singing. I'd like to close this chapter by giving you an overview of how I would combine each element for creating various moods for singing and worship.

Creating an Energetic Atmosphere

Creating an energetic atmosphere allows teenagers to get a little wild and crazy. I've found this helps release excess energy and lower inhi-bitions. At the same time, it unifies them as a group. I'll usually start with two to three really upbeat songs with a fast tempo and a lot of clapping and hand motions. Whether we're in chairs or on the floor, I make sure they get a chance to get up on their feet and interact with one another through the singing time. Touching is important as they come together as a group. Back rubs, hugs, and other antics are great for bringing students together. If students are in chairs, I might have them stand on them or change seats so they interact with different people during the singing.

On the technical side, I suggest having the lights up and the volume loud. You might also want to have students come up front to help lead the songs, too. The focus at this time is purposefully horizontal—namely, celebrating Christian community with one another through the lyrics and actions of the songs.

Creating an Atmosphere for Intimate Praise and Worship

After the energetic songs, I like to soften the mood and move into vertical worship (songs directed specifically about and to God). I've found that low lighting helps calm students and aids in the transition from wild and crazy to soft and intimate. You may also wish to encourage students to hold hands or put their arms around each other during certain songs. By giving them permission to do this, you will encourage an interaction that is quite unifying and meaningful to students.

Another idea is to break your singing up within the program; this method promotes both the wild and crazy and the soft and intimate without having to make difficult transitions. For example, you might begin your meeting with a crowdbreaker or a game, then do your wild and crazy singing, followed by announcements, the talk or small groups, then close with praise and worship. Often I begin our meetings in chairs but close them with students sitting on the floor, where they experience intimate times of singing and sharing.

Singing a cappella or using musical interludes while sharing Scripture verses, prayer requests, praises, or prayer can also create special moods of reflection, togetherness, and intimacy.

Do not neglect to consider the importance that creating the right atmosphere can play in your worship ministry. Knowing how to create the right environment can do as much for student participation as knowing what songs to choose or instruments to use.

THINK ABOUT IT

1. List several practical things you could do with your present meeting room to enhance its atmosphere.

    _____
    _____
    _____
    _____

2. What is your most common seating arrangement during your students' time of singing?

    A) straight rows of chairs
    B) chairs in a circle
    C) chairs in a semicircle
    D) sitting on the floor

3. Try using a variety of seating arrangements during singing times. Start by using one you haven't tried before and see how your students respond.

4. Identify the distractions in your meeting room that make singing more difficult. What could you do to remove or reduce these distractions?

11

VARIETY AND CREATIVITY

I love singing. It makes me feel better about problems I've been having . . . it's sort of like flying. I feel lifted up in a way.

Cynthia—9th grade

I can close out everyone around me and sing praises to the Lord and not worry about what I'm wearing or how well I sing. I can focus on what God has done for me when I sing. One of the parts I look forward to most at church is when we worship God in song.

Sheri—11th grade

If you're a creature of habit, then this chapter is especially for you! Creatures of habit are comfortable with the status quo. They operate on an if-it-ain't-broke-don't-fix-it mentality. After all, providing variety takes time. With everything else that needs to be done in ministry, who has the energy to be creative?

As a result, creatures of habit wonder why their students seem bored or uninterested during times of singing; I know I've wondered that on occasion with my groups over the years. Perhaps you have too. When the same ol' thing is done in the same ol' way with the

139

same ol' people at the same ol' time in the same ol' room, don't be surprised when kids keep expressing the same ol' gripes as they yawn the same ol' yawns.

This chapter will give you several ideas on how to add variety and creativity to your singing ministry that will wake up, encourage, and challenge the troops!

WORSHIP FIELD TRIPS

Ever considered taking your worship ministry on the road? Here are several fun and creative ideas that will both challenge and excite your students.

Worship Your Creator

"Worship Your Creator" is a field trip designed to allow students to experience firsthand the beauty of God's creation. Southern California, for example, contains a wide variety of climates all within a few hours' drive. My friend John Hoppis took a group of high school students on a field trip that included stops at the beach, the mountains, and the desert, all in one day. A trip such as this is an excellent teaching opportunity because it brings students into a keen awareness of God as Creator and shows them the range of His creativity. Singing praises to God around a campfire surrounded by the soothing sensation of the ocean waves, the vitality of a mountain forest, or the solitude of the desert can be an encounter with the Almighty not soon forgotten!

If you don't live in an area where different climates or natural environments are readily accessible, try adapting as best as you can. Visit high places and low places, dry places and wet places, open fields and wooded forests, rocky mountains and flat valleys. Try to visit several contrasting expressions of God's creation in one block of time while providing a creative worship experience for your students through singing.

Visit Churches with Different Worship Styles

You may need to get permission from your senior pastor, church board, or the parents of your students beforehand, but visiting churches with completely different styles of worship can be a rewarding and challenging experience. A friend of mine once brought his all-white, suburban youth group to an all-black, inner-city church. He said at first his students were visibly uncomfortable, yet were soon joining in with the rest of the congregation singing, swaying, and shouting praises to the Lord at the top of their lungs. In fact, they kept right on singing the songs they had learned that night all the way home on the church bus!

You may also want to introduce your students to the way different denominations or traditions sing and worship. I remember one time taking a small group of interested students to a charismatic service (our church had no charismatic worship traditions). Talk about taking a group of kids out of their comfort zones! My students observed people dancing, bowing down, raising their hands, playing tambourines, and participating in a whole lot of other practices they had never seen Christians do before.

We went out for hamburgers afterwards and had one of the most profitable discussions on worship I think I have ever had with a group of teenagers. Not only were they excited about what they had seen, but I think they were more appreciative of their own tradition as a result.

If your church has informal worship practices, take your students to a formal or liturgical church. If they are from a traditional denomination, take them to a contemporary service. This type of exposure can be fun, and it can teach your students much about singing and worship.

Visit Other Youth Groups

For a refreshing change of pace, why not go across town and join another youth group for a time of singing and worship? It shouldn't be too difficult to find another group that meets on the same night as yours. Get together ahead of time with the worship leader from the other group and plan your song lists. Not only will your group get to teach a few of their favorites, but I'm sure they'll learn a few in the process! I've found that getting groups together occasionally for times of worship (and not just for fun activities) enhances student's awareness of the larger body of Christ and communicates unity within our individual diversity.

SINGING IN DIFFERENT LOCATIONS

Ever thought of experimenting with different locations for singing? I've taken my students to a number of locations around the church not only for variety's sake, but to emphasize certain principles in the process. Here are several suggestions you may be able to use or adapt to your own situation.

Church Nursery

If your church nursery is vacant on the night you meet with your students, why not meet there to have a time of singing? Include a devotional on Matthew 18:1-6 (where Jesus teaches on having a childlike faith). Note the difference between a childish (immature, selfish) and a childlike faith. A childlike faith might be characterized by trust, dependence, openness, and an eagerness to learn. Include childhood favorites as well as songs that speak of trust and reliance, such as "You Are My Hiding Place" and "Cares Chorus." Let each student hold a toy or stuffed animal during your time of worship to give them a personal object lesson.

Church Bathroom, Kitchen, Basement, or Gym

Some of you may think to yourselves that a church bathroom or kitchen is a strange place for worship, but there is a point. As I have noted earlier in this book, bathrooms, kitchens, basements, gyms (or other tiled- or hardwood-floor rooms) provide "live" acoustics. Sound comes alive in places like these when used for singing. If you've ever wished your students would sing out a bit more, why not have a short devotional on several of the passages in the Psalms that encourage shouting praises to God! Bring your group to one of these locations, and encourage them to sing at the top of their lungs in praise to the Lord. You may be surprised at how terrific your group will sound . . . and so will they!

Fireside Room

Many churches have a room with a fireplace in it. People love the atmosphere a fire can create. Closeness and intimacy seem to occur naturally as young people begin to open up and share with one another around a fire. In one of my ministries, we offered our students a once-a-month prayer-and-worship time called "G.L.O.W." which stood for "God Loves Our Worship." We met in the fireside room of our church after the evening service and sang praises to God with just our voices and guitars. It became not only one of our students' favorite times, but it provided an opportunity for students to join in and learn to lead worship with their own instruments as well.

Up on the Roof

Does your church have a flat rooftop your kids could sit on safely? If so, why not arrange for your group to meet on the rooftop of a church building? (Get approval from your senior pastor or church board before attempting this!) Put down pillows or plastic tarps for students to sit on so they are at least partially comfortable. Have students look up at the stars and consider God's handiwork and the awesomeness of His majesty and creative power. You may wish to do a devotional out of the first chapter of Genesis or read a Creation Psalm such as Psalm 8 or Psalm 148. Your students will be excited because they will be doing something totally unconventional, yet it will be an evening of worship they will remember for a long time. But please remember: Be careful!

Church Sanctuary

OK, maybe this one seems obvious. But for many students the sanctuary is part of the "grown up" world and not really a place for them to worship. If you can, use the sanctuary one evening for a praise-and-worship time that focuses on humility and reverence before God. Experiment with kneeling (if it is unfamiliar to your students), and sing songs that express our position of humility before God. Scriptures that describe the royal glory and majesty of God would enhance this time of praise.

DEVELOPING THEMES IN SINGING AND WORSHIP

Just as themes for worship are developed for many adult church services, so too can they be developed for youth worship. Typically, a youth song session is comprised of songs with a variety of messages. While there is nothing necessarily wrong with this, you may want to challenge yourself by selecting material to create themes.

143

For starters, you might consult the subject or topical index in the back of most chorus books. Typically these books will include a variety of themes and list suggested songs accordingly. Themes such as assurance, concern for others, confession, creation, faithfulness of God, forgiveness, humility, holiness, joy, love, the names of God, peace, promises, thanksgiving, unity, and victory are all possibilities to choose from.

Another option is to choose a set of songs that come entirely from the Psalms. Many of today's popular choruses are taken directly from the Psalms, so you shouldn't have any trouble finding material. Be sure to emphasize that the Book of Psalms is *the* songbook of the Bible, filled with encouragements for us to "praise the Lord!"

A variation on this idea is to choose a set of songs taken directly from other Scriptures. For example, I might say to my students, "Let's see how many Scriptures you have memorized. Do you know this verse?" I then reel off several Scripture references and usually get a dumbfounded expression from most of my students. But when we begin to sing the Scripture songs, an awareness and familiarity invariably comes across their faces. When I do a set of Scripture songs, students typically are surprised to discover how much they actually know!

Short devotionals are also effective additions to themed times of worship, and I use them regularly. For example, to illustrate thanksgiving, I might do a short devotional from Colossians 3:15-17. I point out to students several principles of thanksgiving: first, be thankful that the peace of Christ rules in your hearts; second, praise the Lord through song with thanksgiving in your hearts; and third, whatever you do in word or deed, do it in the name of Jesus with thanksgiving.

You might want to include a short story or illustration to complement a devotional passage. Make sure your words add to, rather than detract from, the singing. I am not suggesting that you preach a sermon or message; you need only offer a short thought to enhance the worship experience.

Finally, I like to include what I call "planned spontaneity" in our themed worship times. I encourage students to interject one-sentence prayers to God, interspersed between songs, that deal with our theme. For example, at the beginning of a worship set on the theme of love, I tell students to think of one-sentence reasons why they love God. I then tell them that in the middle of our worship time we will pause to lift up our offerings of love to God. I encourage every student to participate and share their responses out loud in the form of short prayers. One student might say, "I love you, Father, for your patience with me." Or one might share, "I love you, Lord, for your encouragement to me," and so on.

You may experience silence for a while until the first person shares, but soon everyone will be joining in as the "spontaneity" moves from student to student. I've found encouraging this type of spiritual expression, like nothing else we do in our worship times, draws students closer to one another and to the Lord! Other ideas for planned "spontaneity" include sharing thanks, sharing praises, sharing favorite Scriptures, or sentence prayers on any selected subject. To reduce "dead air" and the "intimidation factor," you might want to arrange before the worship time to have two or three students begin this time of sharing.

ENCOURAGING EXPRESSION

A final way to add variety and life to your group's worship experience is to encourage physical expression. Now before those of you from noncharismatic traditions slam the book shut, I encourage you to hear me out. Although I personally do not come from a charismatic tradition, I have become comfortable over the years with the idea and practice of encouraging biblical expression in youth worship. I am not alone in this. Many conservative, evangelical, noncharismatic churches over the past several years have become less inhibited and more accepting of the idea of outward expression in worship.

What's so worshipful about restraining yourself from physical expression, anyway? I've searched the Scriptures in vain trying to locate examples where sitting, slouching, or sleeping were regarded as legitimate expressions of heartfelt biblical praise and worship. What I do find are Scriptures admonishing believers to raise their hands (Nehemiah 8:6, 1 Timothy 2:8; Psalms 63:3-4; 134:1-3; and 141:1-4), to bow down (Nehemiah 8:6; Psalm 95:6-8), to clap their hands (Psalm 47:1), and to shout joyfully (Psalm 32:11; 47:1; 65:13)!

Are your students lifeless when it comes to singing God's praises or worshipping Him with intensity? Perhaps your worship is imbalanced, expressing only certain aspects of your humanity. Richard Foster comments that, "God calls for worship that involves our whole being. The body, mind, spirit, and emotions should all be laid on the altar of worship. Often we have forgotten that worship should include the body as well as the mind and spirit."[1] Likewise, Warren Wiersbe observes:

> If true worship is the response of the whole person to God, then we dare not neglect the emotions. We permit people to express their emotions at weddings, funerals, and athletic events, but not at a worship service. The important thing today seems to be that you mark your Bible and write outlines in your notebook, but whatever else you do, keep your emotions hidden.[2]

After seeing how most of my students enthusiastically respond at their weekend football games, I often encourage them to show the same enthusiasm in their praise and worship. I encourage them to sing and shout in celebration to God as they would at one of their school games.

What about encouraging expression in more intimate ways? I'd suggest starting by having your students actually do what a certain song might be saying. For example, the songs "Thy Lovingkindness" or "In Moments Like These" talk about lifting up hands. Simply give your students permission and the freedom to experiment with lifting their hands in worship. One time we were singing the song "Come Let Us Worship and Bow Down," and I asked my students to get on their knees as we sang the song. What an impact that simple gesture made on that group of inexpressive students!

Remember to be sensitive to your students and respect what they are and are not familiar or comfortable with. Don't push them into worship practices that they are not ready for or that would cause confusion among their parents or the church. As I mentioned in chapter 3, talk to the pastors or elders at your church and get their support. Be sensitive and loving when teaching expression in worship.

THINK ABOUT IT

1. In what ways are you a "creature of habit" when it comes to your worship-leading practices?

2. How open would your church and the parents of your students be to taking your group to observe another church's worship practices? What different kinds of worship traditions do you think your students would appreciate seeing? Which kinds of worship would you like to see your students exposed to?

3. What places in your church might provide your students with a creative worship experience?

4. Prepare a worship theme that you could use for your group. Use the format below to help you get started:
   Theme: _____
   Songs: _____
   Scripture: _____
   Story: _____

5. Search the Book of Psalms and look up as many references as you can that encourage physical expression in one form or another. List them here:

   _____
   _____
   _____
   _____

6. To make yourself more comfortable with outward expression in worship (like raising your hands or kneeling), try this exercise: Sometime at night go outside, raise your hands to the heavens, and simply express to God your thankfulness for the wonder of His creation. In addition, try kneeling for prayer each night before you go to bed for a week. You may find it makes a difference in your prayer life!

CONCLUSION

I had just completed my final music preparations as the students began to arrive for our midweek gathering. They were in good spirits and were busily socializing with one another as the youth room began to fill. I like it when kids are in a good mood—it makes leading them in singing and worship that much more enjoyable. They soon took their seats and were ready for the evenings program. Visitors were recognized, announcements were made, and a crowdbreaker initiated. The group responded enthusiastically, and now it was my turn to lead them in singing. My worship team and I were ready to go!

The lights were up, and we began to jam on our instruments as we opened with a set of upbeat songs. We had several students join us up front to help lead the clapping and hand motions. They did a great job—kids love to see their friends up front! The room was alive, almost out of control, as the group sang out with real enthusiasm. It was tough calming them down and getting them to make the transition into a celebration time of focusing on the Lord. But with a little encouragement (I never use rebuke, although maybe a little admonishing now and then) and softer lighting, I soon had their attention.

With everyone seated, I asked a student to lead the group in prayer. We asked the Lord to help us focus on Him and not our neighbors or anything else that might distract us. During the prayer I had one of my leaders dim the lights, and after the prayer the group seemed more settled and prepared to worship. I shared with them that at some point during our singing we would pause to share with one another spontaneous, one-sentence praises to the Lord, beginning with the words, "Lord, I praise You for _____." The students filled in their own answers to the statement.

We then began our worship set, opening with a new call-to-worship song I had been wanting to teach them. The worship team played the tune as I taught the verses and chorus. We did the song three times to get the students comfortable with it.

We then sang several praise songs. One of them spoke of raising your hands, so I encouraged my students to do just that if they liked. Some of the students raised their hands and some did not, but I did not sense that anyone was made to feel uncomfortable.

We then paused for our short time of one-sentence "praise prayers" to God. Our keyboard player played softly in the background as students began to share. It started out slowly, but soon everyone was involved.

As our sharing time ended, we moved into our final two worship songs. As the last one began, I asked the students to stand and take the hand of the person next to them. We concluded as a unified group, with all God's children saying "Amen!"

Could you picture such a time of singing and worship in your group? I hope so. Not every time goes as well as the one I just described to you, but many of them do. My goal in this book has been to encourage you and hopefully stimulate you to think of singing as more than just something you do at youth group. May your worship times become a meaningful experience that will enable your students to understand God more clearly, know Him more deeply, and walk with him more closely.

POSTSCRIPT

RESULTS OF WORSHIP: STUDENT RESPONSES
As has been stated throughout the book, our central purpose in worship is not to bless ourselves, but to bless God. However, in glorifying our Lord, we ourselves receive blessings and benefits that enrich and enhance our Christian lives.

Although each person's experience with God through worship is personal and, in a sense, unique, throughout my years of youth ministry I have observed several general benefits of worship in the lives of my students:

1. A Christian will be drawn into closer fellowship with God through the communion of His Holy Spirit in worship.
2. Worship provides an opportunity for the Holy Spirit to draw and convict unbelievers as they yield to the Lord in song.
3. During worship, Christian students will be receptive to the Holy Spirit's conviction of sin in their lives.
4. During worship, believers experience through singing a release of anxiety and emotional burdens and sense the peace of God.
5. Worship enables believers to sense the reality of God and His work in their lives.
6. Worship creates a sense of community and fellowship among believers.

I hope you have enjoyed the student comments I have sprinkled throughout the book. I want to close with some more of their words. Worship is a beautiful gift from God that has wonder-working power in our lives. If you don't believe me, listen to these kids. And remember, these could be your kids talking. (These are actual student responses to the question, What affect has worship through singing had on your relationship with the Lord?)

Worship is like saying "thank you" to a friend that's always there for you. That's exactly what it is. After singing these songs I actually even feel better about myself. I guess I realize that I'm praising an awesome God.

Matt—10th grade

I like to sing, but sometimes I feel embarrassed because my voice isn't really the best. But when we have times of worship I try to make everything around me fade and I don't care how good or bad I sing because I'm singing to the Lord and he doesn't care how my voice sounds—just that I'm singing to Him.

Bethany—9th grade

Worship makes me feel so close to God, my family, and my friends. I think it's the greatest feeling you could ever have.

Dianna—7th grade

Worship reminds me of my inadequacies and sinful nature and motivates me to want to live a godly life. Sometimes I imagine myself singing before Him in Heaven one day, praising and worshipping Him. . . . I've also had times where He's tapped on my heart's door and said, "Denise, I've missed spending time with you this week." Those are the times when my worship is most meaningful because I know how much He loves me and forgives me no matter how often I fail Him.

Denise—youth leader

Worship makes me feel a great deal of calm. I can focus in on worshipping through music easier than when I'm at home trying to pray.

Usually I feel close to the Lord whenever I have a praise tune flying through my head.

Robert—12th grade

When we sing it makes me think about all the bad things I did or didn't do and it makes me pray for God's forgiveness.

Vanessa—7th grade

Worship times make me feel close to God. I can express my love to Him. I can feel the greatness of God. I feel his love for us. I feel united with everyone as we worship God together. It reminds me that God is always there for me, and I can thank Him through worship.

Paul—9th grade

Worship makes me feel very good inside. I feel like I am not alone.

James—8th grade

Lots of songs really get through to me. I pay attention to the lyrics and I understand what God has done for me.

Michelle—7th grade

I have realized that even if your parents do not love each other and it affects you, or if you do not feel loved, I know that your Heavenly Father will love you and you can go before Him and thank Him and love Him in worship and praise.

Megan—9th grade

Singing in worship makes me feel really good. It's like God is with us and he sees us worshipping Him. These times of worship make me feel very clean and happy.

Maryann—8th grade

Through the worship time in the youth group I have grown spiritually. The songs we sing stay with me all day and I really like them. I am not by habit a singer, but I feel comfortable singing the praise songs.

David—9th grade

APPENDIX 1

LICENSING AND COPYRIGHT INFORMATION
The companies listed in this appendix will give you access to any and all information you may require for understanding and obtaining proper copyright use.

Christian Copyright Licensing International (CCLI)
6130 NE 78th Ct., Suite C11
Portland, OR 97218-2853
1 (800) 234-2446

For the brochure "Circular 1: Copyright Basics," write to:

The Copyright Office
The Library of Congress
Washington, D.C. 20559
(202) 707-3000

For the brochure "The Church Musician and the Copyright Law," write to:

Church Music Publishers Association (CMPA)
P.O. Box 158992
Nashville, TN 37215
(615) 791-0273

Also, for a fee of $2, CMPA will supply a current listing of all major Christian music copyright holders and publishers. (Please send cash only.)

APPENDIX 2

SLIDE AND TRANSPARENCY COMPANIES
These companies provide prepared slides and transparencies or can custom make them to meet your needs.

Hawks Nest
P.O. Box 92626
Lakeland, FL 33804-2626
(813) 853-4700

Phil Barfoot Music Company
1919 Williams Street
Suite 320
Simi Valley, CA 93065-2859
(805) 520-1740

Christian Slide Service
3260 Broadhaven N.W.
Massillon, OH 44646
(216) 833-3000

Screen Light Visual Communications
7662 Golden Triangle Drive
Eden Prairie, MN 55344
(612) 944-1353

The Praise Project
10419 Roxborough Pk Rd.
Littleton, CO 80125
(303) 791-8174

Graphic Visions
P.O. Box 540459
Omaha, NE 68154-0459
(402) 333-3688

Worship Visions, Inc.
1484-148 Lane N.W.
Minneapolis, MN 55304
(612) 434-8258

My Father's Business
P.O. Box 187
Danville, IN 46122
(317) 745-0409

Appendix 3

A SELECTED LISTING OF YOUTH MUSIC AND CONTEMPORARY PRAISE-AND-WORSHIP COMPANIES
• denotes specifically youth-oriented material

COMPANY	SONG BOOKS	SPLIT TRACKS	SLIDES	TRANS- PARENCIES	AUDIO- CASSETTES
Maranatha! Music P.O. Box 31050 Laguna Hills, CA 92654 (714) 586-5778	✓	✓	✓	✓	✓
Integrity Music 1000 Cody Road Mobile, AL 36695 1 (800) 533-6912	✓	✓			✓
Vineyard Ministries International P.O. Box 68025 Anaheim, CA 92817 1 (800) 852-8463	✓	✓		✓	✓
Benson Publishing Group 365 Great Circle Road Nashville, TN 37228 1 (800) 444-4012	✓	✓			✓
Brentwood Music 316 Southgate Court Brentwood, TN 37027 1 (800) 333-9000	✓	✓	✓		✓
Genevox Music Group 127 Ninth Ave. North Nashville, TN 37234 1 (800) 251-3225	✓	✓			

COMPANY	SONG BOOKS	SPLIT TRACKS	SLIDES	TRANS-PARENCIES	AUDIO-CASSETTES
•Group Books P.O. Box 481 Loveland, CO 80539 1 (800) 747-6060	✓	✓		✓	
•Carport Sound 3015 Moores Lane Texarkana, TX 75503 (903) 831-6000		✓			
•Celebration Ministries P.O. Box 1990 Coppell, TX 75019 (214) 401-0110	✓	✓			
•Songs and Creations P.O. Box 7 Mariposa Ave. San Anselmo, CA 94960-0007 (415) 457-6610	✓				✓
•Cokesbury P.O. Box 801 Nashville, TN 37202 (800) 672-1789	✓	✓		✓	
•High Praise Ministries P.O. Box 23711 Oklahoma City, OK 73123	✓			✓	
•Shepherd Ministries 2845 W. Airport Fwy Suite 137 Irving, TX 75062 (214) 570-7599	✓	✓			

NOTES

Chapter 1

1. Michael Coleman and Ed Lindquist, *Come and Worship* (Old Tappan, N.J.: Fleming H. Revell, 1989), 26.
2. A. W. Tozer, *Worship: The Missing Jewel of the Evangelical Church* (Camp Hill, Pa. : Christian Publications, 1992), 20.
3. Jim Burns, *The Youth Builder* (Eugene, Oreg.: Harvest House, 1988), 104.
4. Richard Foster, *Celebration of Discipline* (New York: Harper Row, 1978), 140.
5. Warren Benson and Mark Senter, III, eds., *The Complete Book of Youth Ministry* (Chicago: Moody Press, 1987), 53.
6. Ibid., 389.

Chapter 2

1. Ronald Allen and Gordon Borror, *Worship: Rediscovering the Missing Jewel* (Portland, Oreg.: Multnomah, 1982), 16.
2. William Temple, *Reading in St. John's Gospel, First Series* (London: Macmillan, 1939), 68.
3. Don Wyrtzen, *A Musician Looks at the Psalms: A Journal of Daily Meditations* (Grand Rapids: Zondervan, 1988), 143.
4. Graham Kendrick, *Learning to Worship as a Way of Life* (Minneapolis: Bethany House, 1984), 22.
5. Foster, *Celebration*, 138.
6. Warren Wiersbe, *Real Worship: It Will Transform Your Life* (Nashville: Oliver Nelson, 1986), 27.
7. Robert E. Webber, *Worship Is a Verb* (Waco, Texas: Word, 1985), 29.
8. Geoffrey Wainwright, *Doxology: The Praise of God in Worship, Doctrine, and Life* (New York: Oxford, 1980), 443.
9. Ralph P. Martin, *The Worship of God: Some Theological, Pastoral, and Practical Reflections* (Grand Rapids: Eerdmans, 1982), 210.
10. D. J. Fant, *A. W. Tozer* (Harrisburg, Pa.: Christian Publications, 1964), 90.
11. Colin Brown, ed., *The New International Dictionary of New Testament Theology,* vol. 2 (Grand Rapids: Zondervan, 1976), 876-77.
12. R. Harris et al., eds., *Theological Wordbook of the Old Testament,*

vol. 1 (Chicago: Moody Press, 1980), 217-18.

13. Ibid., 364-65.

14. James Strong, *The Exhaustive Concordance of the Bible* (Peabody, Mass.: Hendrickson Publishers), 47.

15. R. Harris, *Theological Workbook,* 245.

16. Brown, *Dictionary of New Testament,* 3: 816-17.

17. Ibid., 817-18.

18. C. S. Lewis, *Reflections on the Psalms* (San Diego: Harcourt, Brace, Jovanovich, 1958), 97.

19. Webber, *Worship Is a Verb,* 131.

Chapter 3

1. Charles Kraft, "How Our Worldview Affects the Way We Worship," *Worship Leader*, vol. 1, no. 3 (June/July 1992): 10.

2. Ibid., 53.

3. John Dettoni, "Worship that Fits the Worshipper," *Youthworker Journal* (Spring 1990): 30.

Chapter 4

1. Kendrick, *Learning to Worship*, 154.

2. Jack Hayford et al., *Mastering Worship* (Portland, Oreg.: Multnomah, 1990), 36.

3. Yohann Anderson, *Hot Tips for Song Leaders* (San Anselmo, Calif.: Songs and Creations Inc., 1992), 5

Chapter 5

1. Dennis C. Benson, *Creative Worship in Youth Ministry* (Loveland, Colo.: Group, 1985), 136.

2. Ibid., p. 135.

3. Mike Kinard, *Drums in Worship.* (MK Productions, Garland, Texas.)

4. Todd Hunter, "Building a Worship Team," in *Worship Leaders' Training Manual* (Anaheim, Calif.: Worship Resource Center/Vineyard Ministries, 1987), 110-111.

Chapter 6

1. "Circular 1: Copyright Basics," Washington, D.C.: Library of Congress.

Chapter 7
1. Anderson, *Hot Tips for Song Leaders,* 14.
2. Terry Hall, *Dynamic Bible Teaching with Overhead Transparencies* (Elgin, Ill.: David C. Cook, 1985), 37-41.
3. Dennis C. Benson and Bill Wolfe, *The Basic Encyclopedia of Youth Ministry* (Loveland, Colo.: Group, 1981), 284-286.
4. Barry Liesch, *People in the Presence of God* (Grand Rapids: Zondervan, 1988), 95.

Chapter 8
1. Tom Coomes, *The Worship Leader Workshop* (Laguna Hills, Calif.: Maranatha! Music, 1992), 42-43.
2. Danny Daniels, "Songwriting," in *Worship Leaders' Training Manual,* 120-121.

Chapter 9
1. Coomes, *Worship Leader,* 33.
2. Allen and Borror, *The Missing Jewel,* 92-93.
3. Kendrick, *Learning to Worship,* 155-156.
4. Chuck Smith, Jr., "Leading People to an Encounter with God," *Worship Leader,* vol. 1, no. 4 (August/September 1992): 26.
5. Anne Ortlund, *Up with Worship* (Ventura, Calif.: Regal Books, 1975), 78.

Chapter 10
1. Anderson, *Hot Tips for Song Leaders,* 10-11.
2. Allen and Borror, *Worship: Rediscovering the Missing Jewel,* 181.

Chapter 11
1. Foster, *Celebration of Discipline,* 147.
2. Wiersbe, *Real Worship,* 24.

RESOURCES

Books on Worship

• Allen, Ronald, and Gordon Borror. *Worship: Rediscovering the Missing Jewel.* Portland Ore.: Multnomah, 1982.

• Benson, Dennis C. *Creative Worship in Youth Ministry.* Loveland, Colo.: Group, 1985.

• Coleman, Michael, and Ed Lindquist. *Come and Worship.* Old Tappan, N.J.: Fleming H. Revell, 1989.

• Foster, Richard. *Celebration of Discipline.* New York: Harper and Row, 1978.

• Hayford, Jack, et al. *Mastering Worship.* Portland, Ore.: Multnomah, 1990.

• Hayford, Jack. *The Heart of Praise.* Ventura, Calif.: Regal Books, 1992

• Kendrick, Graham. *Learning to Worship as a Way of Life.* Minneapolis: Bethany House, 1984.

• Liesch, Barry. *People in the Presence of God.* Grand Rapids: Zondervan, 1988.

• Martin, Ralph. *The Worship of God: Some Theological, Pastoral, and Practical Reflections.* Grand Rapids: Eerdmans, 1982.

• Ortland, Anne. *Up with Worship.* Ventura, Calif.: Regal Books, 1975.

• Tozer, A. W. *Whatever Happened to Worship?* Camp Hill, Pa.: Christian Publications, 1985.

• Wainwright, Geoffrey. *Doxology: The Praise of God in Worship, Doctrine, and Life.* New York: Oxford, 1980.

• Webber, Robert E. *Worship Is a Verb*. Waco, Tex.: Word Books, 1985

• Wiersbe, Warren W. *Real Worship: It Will Transform Your Life*. Nashville: Oliver Nelson, 1986.

Magazines
Worship Leader is an excellent bimonthly resource. For subscription information write: *Worship Leader,* P.O. Box 40985, Nashville, TN, 37204 or call (800) 331-8947.

Music Songbooks and Collections
A. Publisher Collections
  1. Maranatha! Music
     • *Praise Chorus Book,* first edition
     • *Praise Chorus Book,* second edition
     • *The Praise and Worship Collection*
     • *100 Hymns/100 Choruses*
     • *Songs for the Congregation,* vol. 1
For information on these titles, write Maranatha! Music, P.O. Box 31050, Laguna Hills, Calif. 92654 or call (714) 586-5778.

  2. Hosanna! Music
     • *Praise Worship Songbooks,* volumes 1-6
       Available from Integrity Music, Inc., 1000 Cody Road, Mobile, AL 36695 or call (800) 533-6912.

  3. Mercy Publishing
     • *Worship Songs of the Vineyard,* volumes 1-3
       Available from Vineyard Ministries International, P.O. Box 68025, Anaheim, CA 92817 or call (800) 852-8463.

B. Other Collections
     • Allen, Dennis. *Power Praise Chorus Book.* Nashville: Genevox, 1992.
     • Anderson, Yohann. *Songs.* San Anselmo, Calif:. Songs and Creations, Inc., 1982.

• Denson, Al. *The Youth Chorus Book,* vols. 1-2. Nashville: Benson, 1990

• Sauer, C., et al. *The Group Songbook.* Loveland, Colo.: Group, 1991

Instrumental and Technical Information
Anderson, Yohann. *Hot Tips for Song Leaders.* San Anselmo, Calif.: Songs and Creations, Inc., 1992.

Chambas, Danny. *Key Training Video.* Oklahoma City: High Praise Ministries, 1992.

Citron, Stephen. *Songwriting: A Complete Guide to the Craft.* New York: Morrow, 1985.

Kraeuter, Tom. *Key to Becoming an Effective Worship Leader.* Hillsboro, Mo.: Training Resources, 1991. To order, call (314) 789-4522.

Owens, Jimmy and Carol. *Words and Music: A Guide to Writing, Selecting, and Enjoying Christian Songs.* Waco, Texas: Word Books, 1987.

Stromberg, Bob. *Get Kids to Sing!* [instructional video] Loveland, Colo.: Group, 1991.

Whitfield, Jane Shaw. *Songwriter's Rhyming Dictionary.* North Hollywood, Calif.: 1974.: 1964.

Secular Trade Magazines
Keyboard (monthly publication). For subscription information write: *Keyboard,* Box 58528, Boulder, CO 80322-8528 or call (800) 289-9919.
Guitar World (monthly publication). For subscription information write: *Guitar World,* P.O. Box 58660, Boulder, CO 80322-8660 or call (303) 447-9330.

Bass Player (bimonthly publication). For subscription information write: *Bass Player,* P.O. Box 57324, Boulder, CO 80322-7324 or call (800) 234-1831.
Modern Drummer (monthly publication). For subscription information write: *Modern Drummer,* P.O. Box 480, Mt. Morris, IL 61054-0480 or call (800) 551-3786.

Biblical Reference Tools
A. General
Strong, James. *The Exhaustive Concordance of the Bible.* Peabody, Mass.: Hendrickson, n.d.

Vine, W. E., *Expository Dictionary of Old and New Testament Words.* Old Tappan, N.J: Fleming H. Revell, 1981.

B. Hebrew Helps
Brown, Francis, et al. *Hebrew-English Lexicon* [coded to Strong's Concordance]. Peabody, Mass.: Hendrickson, 1979.

Harris, R., et al, eds. *Theological Wordbook of the Old Testament,* vols. 1-2 [coded to Strong's Concordance]. Chicago: Moody Press, 1980.

Kohlenberger, John R., ed. *The NIV Interlinear Hebrew-English Old Testament.* Grand Rapids: Zondervan, 1979.

Wigram, George. *The New Englishman's Hebrew Concordance* [coded to Strong's Concordance]. Peabody, Mass.: Hendrickson, 1984.

C. Greek Helps
Brown, Colin, ed. *The New International Dictionary of New Testament Theology,* volumes 1-3. Grand Rapids: Zondervan, 1976.
Berry, George Ricker. *The Interlinear Greek-English New Testament.* Grand Rapids: Zondervan, 1981.

Wigram, George. *The Englishman's Greek Concordance* [coded to Strong's Concordance]. Grand Rapids: Baker, 1979.

ABOUT THE AUTHOR

Jim Marian is the high school pastor at Lake Avenue Congregational Church in Pasadena, California. Jim has been in youth ministry since 1982 and holds a M. Div from Fuller Theological Seminary in Pasadena. CA. and a B.A. in preaching/youth ministry from Pacific Christian College in Fullerton, California.

Jim has led worship for several youth groups and at many camps and conferences. He also speaks to youth workers on various youth ministry subjects, including how to lead students in worship, and is on training team for Maranatha! Music's worship leader workshops. Jim also the author of *Growing Up Christian* (Victor Books). To contact Jim about speaking or conducting a worship leaders seminar in your area, please call Lake Avenue Congregational Church, (818) 795-7221.